Upside Down:

The Paradoxes of Gender in the Twenty-first Century

Deluxe Edition

by Robert L. Waring

Version 1.03

www.upsidedownbook.NET

ISBN-10: 1475292945
ISBN-13: 978-1475292947

For my wife, Elizabeth, who showed me the way.

Table of Contents

Preface

This upside down story began early in the twentieth century when my maternal grandmother, Marguerite Smith Barton,[a] was a key speaker for the women's suffrage movement in England. She later became the first woman to teach public speaking at the Virginia Theological Seminary near Washington, D.C. Curiously, she never mentioned a word of her suffrage work to me, or to any of her other nineteen grandchildren as far as I know. Sadly, her mind's remarkable agility only barely overlapped the dawn of modern feminism. I did not discover her history until well into my adulthood, when pictures of her in a large stylish hat in front of a poster advertising one of her suffrage speeches began to circulate within the family. Part of my motivation for writing this book is to have a conversation with my grandmother about women in society, and to continue something she started more than a hundred years ago.

---

a. My colorful grandmother wore large hats and directed and acted in plays. She read palms, followed astrology, and believed in reincarnation. Armistead Maupin Jr., another of her grandchildren, has described her in greater detail and explained her influence on his success as an author. *See* Gale at 91-93 (Maupin's recollections of his grandmother). Her grandchildren honor her by repeating her favorite Scots blessing: "I'll draw a rosy circle around you." She explained the story of the blessing in a letter discovered after her death:

> There is a Highland legend that when St. Columba made the Holy Christ Circle round anyone, it guarded them from all harm and prospered all their works. The legend goes that St. Columba drew it in the sands, with a cross inside it, bidding the Islanders put it round anyone who worked for good and Christ; and, as he drew, the Circle turned to radiant rose.

As an undergraduate at Princeton in the early 1970's, I saw some of my fellow male students show up at a speech given by feminist Gloria Steinem just so they could walk out in protest. In a William F. Buckley sort of way they thought they were being very amusing, but I could not understand why they went to so much trouble just to be so rude. I was both shocked and embarrassed by their behavior. Why was Steinem so threatening to them?

The energy of the feminist movement pushed through this early resistance, but as a friend of feminism I saw the movement begin to lose its way during the Reagan era. Suddenly it was cool to be reactionary, and that forced feminists to try to redefine their movement to stay relevant. They did not succeed partly because of a brutal internal fight over pornography and prostitution. Bill Clinton rode into office during the year of the woman in 1992 and for a time it seemed that feminism had found new footing. But it fell apart again during the Republican revolution of 1994 and the consequences of Clinton's affair with an intern in what came to be known as Monicagate.

Then came 9/11, which pushed concern for gender equality far into the background, notwithstanding that the terrorism may have been substantially motivated by fears that the spread of Western gender equality would destroy the terrorists' culture of patriarchal dominance. After a decade of marinating in the post 9/11 new normal, feminism seems to have faded into an historical footnote to the presumption that the battle for gender equality has been won. But the viral national discussion about work/life issues prompted by an *Atlantic Magazine* cover story in mid-2012 proved that men and women are still very differently situated in America.[1]

When I started researching this book in 2001, I hoped to show the folly of continued reliance on patriarchy and the importance of adopting feminist principles. After eight years of research and writing, I finally came to the difficult conclusion that among feminism's worst enemies were some of its own goals and values – just as women's worst enemies in puncturing the glass ceiling often are other women. Here was a set of paradoxes worth examining.

As I tried to sort out the puzzle of feminism, I began to more fully appreciate its importance. I realized that gender inequality is crucial to every policy issue we face. This book tries to answer the question: where do we go from here? Should we assume that we will transcend our patriarchal heritage soon? Or, is there a risk that just as women's suffrage lagged behind voting rights for blacks by more than fifty years it may be at least another fifty before a woman is elected to the White House, and much longer than that before women achieve equality by many other measures? If we should try to speed change, what should we do?

*   *

So as not to disappoint any readers, analysis of gender or feminism specifically from a racial or queer (LGBTI) perspective is beyond the scope of this book – although there is a section on gay marriage. But this limitation is not in any way intended to diminish the importance of these viewpoints.

More information about the topics in this book can be found at www.upsidedownbook.NET Reader comments about the book should be posted there or at www.amazon.com/dp/1475292945

Introduction

"Upside down, boy, you turn me, inside out, and round and round." Bernard Edwards and Nile Rodgers[2]

In the early 1970's – half a century after women gained the right to vote – feminism promised to remake the world for women, to create a new cultural landscape where women have complete equality with men. Forty years later, even with the attempted reboot of so-called third-wave feminism, this has not happened. The Equal Rights Amendment to the Constitution ("ERA") guaranteeing equality "on account of sex" was feminism's primary strategy to bring women into a state of parity with men. But its failure to be enacted helped forever taint feminism as a sort of dead language. Only a small minority of women has ever self-identified as feminist, and studies show that women are less happy today than they were in the 1970's.

In many ways progress toward equality is now stalled. Perhaps feminism's inability to achieve many of the goals that shined so brightly forty years ago isn't that it aimed too high, but rather that it lacked a coherent vision and sought too little systemic change beyond the ERA. Columbia University Professor Jane Waldfogel observed that "American feminists made a conscious choice to emphasize equal rights and equal opportunities, but not to talk about policies that would address family responsibilities."[3] An example of this choice is the failure to address the nearly universal need for ceiling-less career tracks that accommodate less than full time employment for extended periods of time.

Further explored in chapter twelve, such a system is an essential step in ending gender discrimination, but cannot be fairly implemented unless it is both gender and purpose neutral.

Yet, many labor under the false illusion that we've largely finished remediating gender inequality in America, when in fact we've barely begun. If the premise that gender conflicts are behind us – propounded in magazines such as *Time* and *The Atlantic*[4] – is false, can we recycle feminism's goal in a new effort? Or should we simply toss feminism on the trash heap of history – like so many other "isms" before it?

Discarding the goals of feminism would be unwise. More than a mere philosophy, feminism has its roots in an immutable characteristic – gender. Its physiological differences can't be blurred by intermarriage the way race and ethnicity can. In the twenty-first century, poverty, war and climate change will compete for our attention as new technologies and social and economic trends come and go. But as *New York Times* columnist Nicholas Kristof asserts, gender inequality is the most important moral issue facing the world.[5] Nearly every policy choice we make today affects gender issues and, more important, vice versa. Through that prism, this book examines how we could restructure society to create a more successful future.

Although this book asserts that remedying gender inequality will benefit us all, its purpose is not to make value judgments about gender differences. I am not saying the world would be a better place if more women were in charge. (But neither am I ruling that out. Part of the discussion in paradox two describes men and women's dissimilar propensities toward violence and war, and there women's attitudes seem preferable.) Women's greater influence and power may bring more societal fairness and diversity of viewpoint and experience. The point of this book and its primary takeaway value judgment, however, is that if we create the conditions that would lead to women's more rapid advancement, *those conditions* (not counting the acceleration mechanisms described in the last chapter) by themselves would make the world a better place.[b]

This book is divided into two parts: Problems and Solutions. As with most public policies, having a deeper understanding of the problems compels the necessity and urgency of the solutions. The Problems section consists of eleven gender paradoxes: realities that were supposed to have changed as a result of feminism, but have not. Examining these paradoxes provides perspective on how the modern women's movement has changed society – or not – forty years on.

Some paradoxes of feminism's legacy are:

*   In the twenty-first century, many measures of women's progress have gone flat.

*   Feminism wasted considerable energy, credibility and political capital spreading the false notion that women are exactly the same as men.

---

b. For example, fairness is good for the economy. A preliminary estimate is that as much as 20% of U.S. economic growth in the past 50 years is the result of increased opportunities for blacks and women. Freeland (citing unpublished study by Chang-Tai Hsieh, Erik Hurst, Charles Jones and Peter Klenow).

[Author's note: The lettered footnotes are optional side paths from the main text. Please only read them if they bring you pleasure, and not if they are too distracting. You can skip them without missing anything critical. The numbered endnotes are citations for those readers who want to see the source material. (For access to web pages that have expired or changed, see www.archive.org, or just search the article title.) Finally, apologies to those readers pining for hyphens; this book adopts a writing style that minimizes their use.]

- Feminism promised that women freed from the sole professional identity of homemaker would be happier, but this has not occurred.

- Feminism promised to make women more assertive, but women still are much less able than men to ask for what they want in the workplace.

- Feminism preached that men stood in the way of women's advancement, but a better characterization is, "We have met the enemy and she is us."

- The goals of feminism have been premised on the false notion that attaining "critical mass" would be the tipping point for monumental change.

- The assumption spawned by feminism was that beauty would matter less, but today it matters as much as or more than it ever has in our networked multimedia world.

- Women are not more in control of their sexuality today.

- Feminism projected that women would safely be able to serve in any job, including the military, but sexual assault still is rampant in the ranks.

- The United States, the birthplace of feminism, is intentionally holding back women's progress around the globe.

- In many areas of Asia, there has been no letup in the pervasive abortion and infanticide of girls in favor of sons.

In spite of its imperfections, it would be a mistake to blame feminism exclusively for these paradoxes and for our failure to remedy gender inequality. Collectively, we must also accept this responsibility. Perhaps one of the reasons for feminism's stagnation in post 9/11 America has been an emphasis on, or perhaps an obsession with, the manly art of fighting terrorism and waging war, reinforcing the notion that men need to be in charge to protect women from harm.[6] A longer term reason why feminism's original goals remain so elusive is that we did not build a national consensus that ending gender inequality is essential to our national cornerstone: freedom. Part of the difficulty in building such a consensus is that culturally and politically, Americans have an aversion to planning anything that smacks of long-term "social engineering."

The perspectives of our "forefathers" shaped many of our national approaches to public policy. One part of that legacy is that our Constitution provided no rights to women. In Thomas Jefferson's *The Declaration of Independence*, only men were "created equal" and had "unalienable" rights to "Life, Liberty and the pursuit of Happiness." But the short term perspective of many of our forefathers is just as important to understanding the public policy myopia that today impedes achieving gender equality. Our forefathers staged their revolution against colonial rule with little experience in social stability, and some had a decidedly pessimistic opinion about planning. Jefferson expressed a popular view that a revolution every generation (twenty years) would help keep government and society vibrant and honest.[7] Our third President's ideas on revolution remain popular with today's Tea Party movement.

Seldom is there public discourse today about how U.S. society will function fifty, twenty or even ten years hence. Politicians almost never look beyond eight years – the term limits for officeholders in many states and for the U.S. President. Our national myopia often is attributed to a fear of "big government."

But we're not afraid of government that builds big things. We often can get it together to build bridges, airports, aircraft carriers or even a space station intended to last decades, but we balk at public policy projects requiring such time frames. There are occasional bursts of collective will triggered by widespread social unrest, such as the Great Depression or the Civil Rights Movement. (But serious efforts toward racial equality began only after bold action by the Supreme Court and the assassination of the President.) Once the unrest has subsided, the collective consensus for planning change is abandoned. One reason why President Obama's heath care reform was so controversial and fell short of its aspirations was that projected cost savings would not reduce expenditures until ten years out – a time frame outside the comfort zone of many Americans.

Our roots as a capitalist democracy reinforce our faith in "market forces" that arise from an uncontrollable mass of individuals – the so-called "wisdom of the crowd."[8] The mass should not and cannot be controlled, so why plan? This cultural maxim was followed by Secretary of Defense Donald Rumsfeld, who insisted that you can't plan how things are going to go – you just have to react to events as they happen. "Freedom's untidy" and "stuff happens," he famously said in the aftermath of the U.S. invasion of Iraq.

In 2010, Fox News Host Glenn Beck drove a sixty-five year old anti-planning screed by economist F.A. Hayek to the top of the best seller list.[c] That same year, the hot new capitalist buzzword was *disruptive* – meant to describe any innovation that revolutionizes existing technology.[9] Columnist David Brooks

---

c. Hayek, THE ROAD TO SERFDOM. This was ironic, because Hayek later wrote, "I doubt whether there can be such a thing as a conservative political philosophy. Conservatism may often be a useful practical maxim, but it does not give us any guiding principles which can influence long-range developments." Hayek, *Why I Am Not a Conservative.*

attempted to give the term some historical context, criticizing social engineering and praising "the vibrancy of the market, the mobility of the people and the disruptive creativity of the entrepreneurs. This vibrancy grew up accidentally...."[10]

But has our adoration for revolution and disruption blinded us to the benefits of planning? Our faith in uncontrollability caused the global economic collapse of 2008. Engaging in public policy planning and having a vibrant, market based economy are not mutually exclusive. Planning in and of itself will not end the American way of life, but failing to plan might. And feminism is unlikely to achieve its potential without national planning.

There is another self-reinforcing mechanism in our faith in uncontrollability. Since we expect good things to happen because of the inherent wisdom of the crowd, we tend to think that whatever goes wrong must be due to individuals' errors, not the flaws in our institutions. This explains the quest to find individuals or particular groups to blame for the Great Recession that began in 2007, rather than planning major reforms of the regulatory system to prevent another meltdown.

Our love of societal untidiness has found its way into gender issues. It's no surprise that a number of books responding to sluggish or negative social trends for women in 2009 were self-help books. These books place the responsibility for solving societal problems women experience squarely on individual women. If your job won't allow you any time for your family, says *Womenomics*, tell your employer he can't survive without you and demand a reduced schedule.[11] If you are unhappy because you're stretched too thin, discard some of your responsibilities, suggests *Find Your Strongest Life*.[12] It seems to have gone out of fashion to argue that the system is at fault,[13] or that our priorities related to gender are the problem.

The Solutions portion of this book proposes societal changes to foster women's advancement. Chapter twelve discusses how, if we want women to take on more leadership roles in business and politics (leaving the *if* to the reader), we should offer them mentors and better part time work and childcare options. Chapter thirteen describes media campaigns that would encourage women to empower themselves and men to support that transformation. To globalize these changes we also need to work much harder to reduce the risk and incidence of rape, and to formally acknowledge the rights women enjoy in Western democracies as the de facto standard the world over.

Beyond these suggestions, chapter fourteen offers another reason why we seem to be experiencing a societal glass ceiling in the U.S. – evidenced by so many indicators of women's participation in leadership having hit a plateau in the new century. Until we align some of our public policy priorities with those the public believes match women's leadership expertise, there may not be the political will to elect larger numbers of women to important public offices. Militarism is a prime reason why men – the warriors – often are favored as leaders.

An example of why women leaders typically are not as valued is our choice not to do what it takes to be one of the best places in the world to be a mother. The U.S. ranked twenty-eighth globally in 2010 – behind such countries as Croatia, Hungary and Slovenia.[14] But, Finland, Iceland, Norway, New Zealand and Sweden ("FINNZS") were among the world's seven best nations to be a mother that year according to Save the Children.[15] Not coincidentally, these five nations are also those where women have the most influence and greatest participation in government leadership.[16] Women's interests and aptitudes are more highly valued in elective offices in these democracies in part because of national focus on optimizing their policies toward motherhood. Where that is not the focus, women's leadership seems less important.

Chapter fourteen also discusses how gay marriage is a sort of canary in a coal mine. When gay marriage is alive and thriving and we've stopped clinging to outdated gender roles in our conception of marriage, we will be ready to eliminate gender inequality throughout our society.

If someday we've implemented the suggestions and realignments described here and women's participation in public office still needs a boost, the final chapter outlines a quota system for state legislatures. Quotas for women, though controversial in the U.S., are successfully in use in the vast majority of the world's democracies.

There is urgency to these suggestions. Paradox two examines strident criticism of feminism for the political rather than scientific position it has taken on gender differences. The predominant feminist assertion has been that cognitively and behaviorally, there are no differences between the genders. But if that is not true, it means that many women fight their instincts and instead force themselves to behave like men to succeed in what still is very much a man's world – one in which patriarchy designed most leadership positions to optimally function with male attributes. If we don't respond to these paradoxes and make some of the societal changes suggested here – especially those in chapter twelve – one possibility is that placing more women in positions designed for men and forcing their partial defeminization may actually reduce the influence of women. It's been said metaphorically that female and male energy reside on opposite sides of a fulcrum and counterbalance each other. If that's an apt analogy, in striving to attain gender equality perhaps we should recognize the value of that balance and take care not to lose it.

These paradoxes define how and why feminism has not succeeded and why systemic changes are needed if gender inequality is to be remedied. Each paradox may resonate differently with different readers. To help guide your journey, you are invited to join a reading group of sample readers with different agendas and interests. Here is a description of how the other members have focused their approaches to the book:

Steve is a twenty-four year old legislative assistant to a congresswoman from a Midwestern state. In his wonkish way, he wants to learn more about the relationship between gender and public policy. He has aspirations to run for public office himself someday, but realizes he does not understand the needs and desires of women voters.

Inga, in her thirties, has a masters in public health administration. An enthusiastic supporter of Hillary Clinton's Presidential campaign, she was disillusioned about the prospects for women's advancement after Hillary's defeat. She is hoping to restore her hope. She also is trying to decide if she wants to marry her partner of three years and have children. She worries that she'll have to choose between having a family and a career.

Diane is a forty-something professional who came of age in the first wave of women graduates of a formerly all-male college. She had no mentors for how to dress, speak to peers and clients, and promote herself in business. As she approaches her professional peak, she feels uncomfortable being complicit in a patriarchal, family unfriendly workplace dynamic and wants to change the game. She is also the mother of three girls, ages ten, fourteen and sixteen, and is looking for guidance about the advice she should be giving them as they form priorities for their adult lives.

Diane's father, Ed, a manager in a technology company, is mainly reading this book because his daughter urged him to, but he supervises a few younger women and admits he does not understand many of their professional needs. Having lived through the bra burning days he thinks feminists have a radical agenda, and wonders if that has changed in recent years.

For all the members of this reading group paradoxes one, two, three, five, six and ten are essential reading, because the Solutions directly rely on them. Bearing this in mind, Steve skips paradox four, that women are not assertive, because in his world they are. But in Ed's, by contrast, they are not, so four is especially interesting to him. Steve also skips seven, about women's beauty still mattering, because he does not see that as a political issue. Inga does not read nine, about women in the military being raped, because she has no plans to enlist. One of Diane's daughters is considering a military career, so she reads it with considerable alarm. Ed does not care much about Asian affairs, so he does not explore eleven, about how abortion and infanticide of females in Asia are increasing. As the fifth member of the reading group, how you choose to read this book is up to you.

Defining the terms sex, power and equality:	When you see the word *sex* printed on the page, what comes to mind? Unless you are a monk, or perhaps especially if you are a monk, you may think carnally. Although an array of issues related to gender stem from sexual relations, sex distracts many people from engaging in a serious discussion of gender relations. There is a lot about gender in this book, and also a lot about sex. So that everyone is on the same page, *gender* used here means gender, while *sex* relates to the activities about which we don't tell young children.

Isn't *power*, to the extent that it connotes domination, a patriarchal term? Many have argued that women are much less interested in power than men are, and greater *influence* may more accurately describe the aspirations of many women rather than attaining power for its own sake. However, influence could for some suggest a more submissive posture that by itself may fail to elevate women out of a secondary role in the outcome of important public policy debates. For lack of better shorthand terms to describe the aspirations of women leaders, this book often uses the terms power and influence synonymously.

But if one defines women's advancement through power and wealth, does that make it a patriarchal construct? If the goal is to displace patriarchy, shouldn't it be done using an alternative framework built on distinct concepts? Perhaps, but the undeniable fact is that society's resources are valued, controlled and transferred by powerful individuals and institutions. Such allocations likely will continue to define public policy for the remainder of this century. Just as the green revolution must succeed in the economic marketplace if it is to succeed as a value system, so must women be an equal influence in resource allocation if they are to gain equality in all aspects of society.

Theresa May, Conservative Party British home secretary, in 2010 decried the use of the word *equality*, calling it a "dirty word" meaning "equality of outcome," where "everybody gets the same out of life, regardless of what they put in."[d] She scrapped the government's effort to reduce inequality and replaced it with the goal of *fairness*, which she defined as "equality of opportunity."[17] On the surface, a focus on process over result could be pragmatic. But May also acknowledged that fairness is a vague term in the context of equality.[18] May and others opposed to government regulation probably prefer fairness to equality in part because it's harder to enforce.

Redefining equality as fairness also fits comfortably with the view of those that assert we have fairness right now. Most positions in government and business are filled on merit, they say, and the reason why women are not in greater numbers in leadership positions is that there are a fewer women than men with sufficient experience willing to make the time commitment required for these positions.

---

d. Gentleman. May failed to note the Orwellian irony of her definition of equality, a term that originally was synonymous with efforts to rectify the plight of the disadvantaged. Speaking to her political base, she complained that those who are not disadvantaged – and previously had no interest in being equal to the general population – now saw themselves as less fortunate, because equality "is available to others, and not to them." Gentleman.

This book harmonizes the two terms. If fairness means the steps that are needed to attain equality in representation, with fairness still a goal until equality is achieved, then for most purposes fairness and equality are interchangeable.

PART ONE: The Problems

Paradox 1: Women's Progress Went Flat.

“ “ The End of Men," proclaimed an *Atlantic Magazine* cover
story in 2010. A modern economy less reliant on manual
labor and better suited to women's skills, combined with
young women's more disciplined approach to higher education,
led to the conclusion that male dominance is passé. The acid test,
according to the article? Procreating American couples'
increasing preference for daughters over sons.[19]

“10 Reasons the Battle of the Sexes is Over," screamed a *Time
Magazine* headline that same year. *Time's* support for this
assertion? A poll that found that three-quarters of men now
believe that having women in the workforce is a good thing, and
deny that to be taken seriously on the job women should be more
like men. Slightly more men than women said that marriage is
very important. Nearly ninety percent of both genders said they
“are comfortable with the notion of a family in which a woman
earns more than a man," and nearly sixty percent said mothers
can be just as productive as fathers at work.[20]

But the same poll found that almost seventy percent of women
believe “men resent women who have more power than they do."
Only about a third of men “strongly agree that a woman can have
a fulfilling life without marriage," but it's a firm majority for
women. And close to a majority of people agreed that men have a
better life than women.[21] Though women may have made
progress since the birth of feminism, this poll shows that many
issues remain to be solved. The lack of progress on many fronts

in the twenty-first century may instead foretell the end of the promise of gender equality.

Some of feminism's key complaints have been about equal pay for equal work, and equal representation in leadership positions. In making claims that the battle was over, *The Atlantic* and *Time* ignored three key signs of stagnant inequality in the U.S. First, the median annual wage that full time women workers were paid at the beginning of the twenty-first century as a percentage of the same wage measurement for men remained virtually unchanged at the end of a decade – at seventy-seven percent.[22] Second, occupational gender segregation – the overall presence of women and men in various professions dominated by one gender – did not change at all in the U.S. between 1996 and 2010.[23] That astounding fact has gone virtually unnoticed. And third, the percentage of women in upper management, director and partner positions, and in many elective offices so far in the new century has remained flat. Feminism has hit a glass ceiling in the workplace. As we'll see, that's paradoxical given where things were supposed be after forty years of effort.

Show Me the Money

A 2003 *Business Week* cover story described the progress women have made in high school and college, surpassing men by many measurements.[24] Even though women do not do as well on standardized tests such as the Scholastic Aptitude Test, by the end of the decade they were earning nearly sixty percent of all U.S. Bachelor of Arts degrees and still climbing. They were obtaining more than forty percent of graduate business degrees.[25] At the top colleges, and at law and medical schools, women outnumbered men.[26] For the first time, more than half of those earning doctoral degrees were women. As *Business Week* observed, women have been working harder in school because they "have to be better to be equal – to make the same money and get the same respect as a guy."[27]

But despite working harder in school, paradoxically women still make less money than men. A study estimated that a woman who had recently graduated from college in 1984 and worked full time earned an average total of 440,000 dollars less than a recent male graduate during their first twenty years in the workforce. The nearly half million dollar disparity was attributed to career choices, delayed career advancement due to taking time off for family, and outright discrimination.[28] This study only measured average earnings of those actually employed at various intervals during those two decades, and thus did not reflect additional income lost by women when they took time off for family.

The average gender pay gap for workers without a four-year college degree has slightly narrowed since the mid-1990s, in part due to effects of the Great Recession described below. Surprisingly, the gap has widened for those with degrees.[29] For example, a study of doctors' salaries in New York State in first jobs after residency eliminated the effects of inflation, hours worked, practice settings, and specialty choices. It found a $3,600 annual gap between men and women in 1999, but a much larger gap of $16,819 in 2008.[30] In Britain's National Health Service, the gender pay gap in 2009 was $24,000.[31] No one predicted that the gender gap would increase for those with the highest levels of education.

Although the aggregate effect of these opposite trends narrowed the average gender pay gap across all occupations by a few percentage points in the first decade of the new century, the *median* annual gender pay gap for full time workers reduced by less than one percentage point, despite much greater progress in earlier decades.[32] The median is the income of that man (or woman) whose income is greater than the lowest half of those workers in his (or her) respective gender, and also less than the higher half. (Given that a relatively small number of those at the top of the income ladder earn very high wages, the average income is higher than the median.) One explanation for the stagnation in the median gap is that even though women made up fifty percent of the total workforce in 2011, they remained stuck at sixty percent of those in low wage jobs.[33] But even the brief achievement of parity would soon backslide, and leave women workers in the minority again.

One might see some progress in the fact that while women lost the most jobs in the recession of 2001,[34] men held more than three-quarters of the jobs lost during the Great Recession.[35] But a *New York Times'* analysis gave feminists little cause for comfort. First, it said the Great Recession hit male dominated industries such as finance and construction the hardest. *The Times'* second explanation went straight to the heart of the earnings paradox: because of the wage disparity between men and women, women were in greater demand in the Great Recession because they are willing to work for less than similarly qualified men.[36] By mid 2011, economic forecasts in both Britain and the U.S. accurately projected that public sector layoffs caused by the recession would increase women's overall unemployment even as private sector jobs began to recover, because women hold a large majority of public sector jobs. In addition, opposite trends in unemployment rates by gender combined with public sector pay cuts and freezes would exacerbate the wage gap rather than narrow it.[37]

The problem of occupation choice in equal pay efforts:

It is well known that the types of occupations women tend to choose are less well compensated than the types men chose. But why? Generally women prefer jobs that focus on people, and are less drawn to jobs where the work is about inanimate things.[38] But is engineering really more difficult to master and perform than teaching or social work, for example, or of greater social or economic value? There is much evidence historically that the jobs women have been drawn to paid less simply because they mostly were held by women. But given that jobs in higher paying fields such as science, technology and engineering do pay better than many others, why does money not motivate more women to enter them today? Is the work itself in traditionally male professions that aversive to women? Do women perceive the work environment as hostile? In some of these fields gender ratios are slowly improving and in a few ratios are worsening. But, in part because jobs in male dominated professions have grown more than in those largely held by women, there has been no overall change in the gender ratios across the various male dominated professions in the new century.[39]

One reason the skewed ratios are difficult to change is quite subtle according to a 2010 report entitled *Why So Few?* It's illustrated by the self-fulfilling prophecy of the myth of women's inability to master advanced mathematics.[40] A seminal experiment, later validated by hundreds of other studies, tested two groups of undergraduates with high math skills. In the group told that men are inherently better at math, men scored an average of twenty-five while women scored just five. Women in the group told both genders perform the same scored an average of seventeen as compared to the men's nineteen.[41] The pervasiveness of the notion that women are not as skilled in math and science helps explain why fewer young women choose those fields.[42] But even if women's self confidence can be boosted, their entry may still be discouraged by the lingering cultural association of science, technology and engineering and mathematics ("STEM") with men.[e]

e. Take a test and see for yourself: https://implicit.harvard.edu.

There is yet another reason for pessimism. The wage gap used to be thought of as a pipeline problem: simply increase the flow of women toward various higher paying careers and the wage gap should disappear, was the thinking. But the life sciences, involving study of living organisms and the most attractive of STEM careers to women, present a case against relying on a pipeline solution. Although "women have toiled in large numbers for decades" in the life sciences, a survey in 2001 found that women there made only seventy-seven percent of what men earned.[43] Even taking into account that on average men were further along in their careers, worked longer and more of them were physicians, still left "significant income disparities."[44] Speaking to this result, the President of the Board of the American Association for the Advancement of Sciences observed, "If you go back 30 or 40 years, the number of graduate students in the life sciences was about equal between the sexes. That being the case, you would expect [salaries] would be equal throughout the spectrum of career positions at this point."[45] But they are not.

Except as noted, all cartoons reprinted by permission of Women's eNews.

A larger question looming over wage differences is how to define gender discrimination. In explaining wage disparities, social scientists often distinguish discrimination from the effects of job choice and inhibited careers due to leaving the workforce for family responsibilities.[46] But the perverse practice of underpaying certain occupations heavily favored by women and the failure of government and business to accommodate women's family obligations is merely an indirect form of discrimination. It may affect women's earnings more than the direct biases of setting women's hiring salaries lower than men's within the same occupation, or offering women raises and promotions less often than men. By focusing on the most obvious discrimination and not asserting a comprehensive approach to remedy all forms of discrimination, feminism has short-changed women.

Show Me the Opportunity

By one report the percentage of managerial and professional jobs held by women doubled from 1980 to 2010 to more than fifty-one percent,[47] but many of the numbers during that last decade tell a story of stagnation. In 2010, a General Accountability Office study examining the most recent data found that between 2000 and 2007 the percentage of women managers grew by only one percent.[48] And growth at the top was flat in the first decade of the new century. In 2002, fewer than sixteen percent of corporate officers in Fortune 500 companies were women, and women held just ten percent of the positions with direct responsibility for profit and loss.[49] In 2008, it was just the same.

Although there was some progress in the number of women on boards of directors in the first half of the decade, there was very little in the last half. As of 2006, women remained less than fifteen percent of the board directors for Fortune 500 companies, and less than two percent of their CEOs. Nearly half of these companies had just one woman or no women on their boards.[50]

Stung by criticism for their lack of diversity, by 2008 eighty-seven percent of Fortune 500 companies had at least one woman on their boards.[51] But given that the overall percentage of women on boards barely changed, this was not progress but rather merely reshuffling the deck. The total number of board positions decreased slightly during this period, which means that for every company that added a woman, another with at least two on its board dropped one. By 2011, the percentage of women board members in the Fortune 500 rose by just one point to sixteen percent, and women CEOs were at just over two percent. Stanford Law Professor Deborah Rhode estimated that in the United States "it will be almost three centuries before women are as likely as men to become top managers in major corporations."[52] In the European Union women fared even less well, with women fewer than ten percent of the board directors of major corporations in 2008,[53] but that's changing as some countries adopt quotas as described in paradox six.

It's probably not a coincidence that law firm management shows similar percentages. In 1985, forty percent of the nation's law students were women, but a survey in 1999 found that only sixteen percent of the partners in the one hundred largest American law firms were women.[54] Surely things had improved by 2009 when the percentage of female law students had risen to forty-seven percent? Not a chance.[55] (Some reports show an increase of three to four percentage points over those ten years largely by including non-equity partners,[56] a new category of salaried partners not sharing in firm profits that contains a higher percentage of women and did not exist in 1999.)

Show Me the Power

Because of Hillary Clinton and Sarah Palin's historic bids in the Presidential race, and Nancy Pelosi's unprecedented ascendency to Speaker, some believe that women made significant gains in elective politics in twenty-first century America. But the sad truth is that women's hold on political power in the U.S. seems by some measures to no longer be increasing and may even be declining. The proportion of women in elected statewide offices, including governors, peaked in 1999, but by 2008 had shrunk to twenty-three percent – its lowest level since 1994. It fell half a percent lower still in 2010.[57] Between 2008 and 2011, the percentage of women governors shrank from sixteen to twelve percent. In 2008, women were mayors in only eleven of the one hundred largest American cities, a drop of four percentage points from just a few years before. The proportion of women mayors in American cities of at least 30,000 persons was less than sixteen percent in 2008, down five percentage points from 1999.

Female representation in state legislatures basically flatlined at twenty-three percent starting in 1999.[58] A single percentage point spike from 2007-2010 collapsed after Republican Party gains in the 2010 election. That's too bad, because if the rate of increase in the percentage of women in state legislatures between 1973 and 1993 had continued at over seven percent per decade, gender parity would have been attained by about 2035. At the 1999-2011 pace, parity is still more than 130 years away. (Women's participation in state legislatures is discussed in more detail in chapter fifteen.)

The U.S. is falling behind most other nations in female representation in national legislatures. In 1997, the U.S. ranked forty-first.[59] By 2009, the U.S. had slipped to seventy-fourth.[60] At this rate, the U.S. could be at the bottom of the rankings in just two decades. After the 2010 elections, the number of women in the U.S. Congress dropped for the first time since 1979.[61]

A substantial part of the reason why women are underrepresented in public office in the U.S. is that it has only been since the 1990s that women have been encouraged to enter this traditionally male club. Prior to that time, women faced high hurdles in garnering endorsements and raising money. But now it seems a key issue is women's lack of enthusiasm for the process. Columnist Joan Ryan, one of many voices bemoaning the stagnation in women's involvement in elective office, opined, "Perhaps the biggest problem in getting more women in office is that too many women don't see it as a problem."[62]

According to one study of elected officials, the percentage of women of all ages who decided to run for office on their own initiative was less than one-third of the percentage of men who made that choice, while the percentage of women who were pushed by someone else to make the plunge was twice as high as the percentage of men.[63] Women are much more likely than men to need someone to tell them it's okay to take the leap.[64] This finding seems consistent with the 2008 personality study spanning fifty-five cultures that found that men in progressive societies respond to new opportunities more than women do.

Women's underrepresentation in elective office is even more severe in the pipeline of young politicians. In 2002 only fourteen percent of all elected officials in the U.S. age thirty-five or younger were women.[65] In 2003, there were nineteen men in Congress under the age of forty and only one woman. In early 2010, there were no women in Congress under forty. None. In the San Francisco Bay Area, described as the "feminist capital of the world," there were fewer women in state and local elective offices in 2008 than there were in 2005. As older women are forced out of politics by term limits, younger women simply are not there to replace them. Factors behind this reversal include women increasingly not wanting to enter politics until after their children are teenagers and having an aversion to the rancor and loss of privacy in political life.[66]

It's ironic that in the fourth decade of the modern women's movement many indicators of women's participation in government and business are flat, and some are negative. Building on prior efforts, nearly all these indicators should at this point be climbing. But they're not. Why should this matter? My work with the California State Legislature showed me what research has confirmed in other states and nations: as the number and power of women legislators have grown, they have enacted more bills benefiting families and children than their male colleagues.[67]

In 2007, a cable television show called *Mad Men* became a cultural phenomenon and critical success. It depicted American culture in the 1960's with stark realism. Unbelted children jumped up and down in the back seats of moving cars driven by their housewife mothers, while fathers worked in offices where women rarely rose beyond the ranks of secretary or janitor. Teenagers and twenty and thirty-somethings viewing the show could appreciate how much life has changed for women since then, yet still fail to understand the arc of that change. Not having witnessed the change across many decades, younger viewers could not see that the tremendous gains made by women in the nineteen seventies and eighties and even nineties began to flatten out in the new century. Assuming that social change over the past four or five decades has been linear may create an unrealistic expectation that change will continue at that prior rate in the future without any additional push to keep things going.

Social conservatives may respond by asserting that women's plateaued participation reflects the natural order, and that most women naturally want to be mothers and tenders of the home fires. Put another way, we may have hit a ceiling because there is presently a limit on how many women are willing to let their careers force them to play a subordinate role in raising their children, or to have no children.[68] In fact, the 2010 *Time* poll found a majority of Americans believe men should work while women stay home with the children.[69] I make no value judgments either way, but note that this finding suggests that women's participation in power in our existing patriarchal social structures may be stretched to capacity. As *The New York Times* noted in early 2012, "women's forward strides in politics and the economy appear to have stalled."[70] If greater women's participation is desirable, we've got to think outside the box we seem to be in.

Paradox 2: Men and Women Are Not the Same.

"Question everything." Heather Ruth Wishik[71]

One of the most surprising aspects of feminism paradoxically also characterizes right wing conservatism: ignoring established science if it contradicts the political agenda. The predominant voices that arise from the feminist chorus say that, except for a few anatomical differences, men and women are exactly alike. A minority voice, "cultural" feminists, attributes gendered behavioral variations to innate differences between the genders sometimes amplified by cultural task roles favoring certain skills. But most feminists insist that apparent differences between men and women are purely a product of women's subordination in a repressive patriarchy, and should gradually disappear as women rise to a more equal footing with men.[f] But why would a movement predicated on social acceptance of modern values paradoxically reject broad scientific findings?

---

f. Kimmel. For example, some linguists attribute gender differences in communication style and language usage to culturally imposed dominant and subordinate gender roles, rather than to any innate gender characteristics. *See* Tavris at 300. One critic of cultural feminism complains, "Far from being benign, the distinctive moral voice [of women] may be an unhealthy adaptation to subjection.... [A]n ethic forced upon women cannot be feminist." Baer at 46-47.

The story of modern ("second-wave") feminism began with the political decision to foreclose arguments about women's inferiority. Thus,

discussion of innate gender differences in behavior or aptitude became antithetical to the women's movement.[72] In *The Female Brain*, author Dr. Louann Brizendine says that "mandatory unisex," a feminist prohibition on acknowledging gender differences, arose in the 1970s.[73] Flash forward three decades later and feminism is stuck in this unisexist rut. In 2005, the President of Harvard University faced a firestorm for suggesting that women's under-representation at the top of university math, science and engineering faculties might be due in part to gender differences in aptitude and in willingness to work grueling hours.[74] Aside from whether he had his facts right,[75] some of his critics asserted that his even raising the issue damaged all women in academia and business. A published essay by the Presidents of Stanford, MIT and Princeton loudly complained that speculation about innate differences "may rejuvenate old myths and reinforce negative stereotypes and biases."[76]

At the close of the first decade of the twenty-first century *The Economist* chimed in, excoriating the acceptance of innate gender differences as immoral and counterproductive. It advised women to ignore the siren voice of what it labeled the "new feminism" and instead follow the example of women leaders such as iron lady Margaret Thatcher, who behave like men and "never admit mistakes."[77] *The Economist's* advice should serve as a warning that failure to examine gender differences may consign us to remain stuck in a patriarchal world based on old stereotypes about men.

The predominant feminist view that men and women are the same is not supported by science, and now is holding back the women's movement.[78] Nearly all of the scientific community accepts that there are significant genetic influences on cognitive, behavioral and personality differences between men and women.[79] Dr. Brizendine, for example, notes that differences in brain function affect what each gender tends to think is important.[80] One of the reasons for this is that huge gender differences in hormones create unique brain chemistries. A very rapidly developing area of neuroscience is mapping the effect of gender based structural and chemical differences in how the brain processes information and emotion.[81]

So why would feminists, while criticizing patriarchy and its institutions, contend that women are just like men? Obviously this makes it easier to argue that they should have the same privileges and opportunities. But the erroneous notion of sameness oversimplifies the issues. Rectifying gender inequality is far more complicated than just forcing societal institutions to treat men and women alike. It's a paradox that feminism responded to old myths and stereotypes about women's inferiority by creating new myths and stereotypes about women's eventual uniformity with men.

What's the Difference?

A consequence of this paradox is another one with even more profound implications: feminism's predominant view that culture, not biology, creates different cognition, behaviors and personalities for men and women. This belief is also incorrect, and has led the women's movement astray. There's plenty of evidence that culture mostly has acted to keep men and women behaving the same, rather than allowing them to act and think differently – as "nature" apparently intended.

Modern feminism's assumption that gender differences would fade under more egalitarian social mores was put to the test in a 2008 global personality study spanning fifty-five cultures. Researchers wondered: how are gender differences changing as patriarchal oppression lessens in progressive countries? It's shocking but true – average personality differences are increasing. As gendered cultural influences lessen, innate differences between men and women influence personality to a greater extent. This confirms previous findings based on multiple studies that gender differences in personality are smallest in the most traditional cultures and greatest in those that are the most modern, affluent and progressive.[g]

These conclusions are contrary to the socialization (blank slate) theory of gender differences long favored by most feminists, which presumed that boys and girls enter the world with similar cognitive and behavioral tendencies and that subsequent personality differences are attributable to the rigid gender roles found in most cultures.[82] The concerns of traditionalists who

---

g. Schmitt, David; Costa; Tierney. These studies assess personality by asking people to answer dozens of standardized survey questions by using a 1-5 scale to rate themselves. The tests measure an array of traits, but in order to compare one group of respondents to another psychologists typically distill the results into a widely accepted index – the most common being the Big Five traits: openness to experience, conscientiousness, extraversion, agreeableness and neuroticism (known by acronym "OCEAN"). The studies try to control for how people in various cultures might differently interpret survey questions. The Big Five index has proven to be predictive of a person's work performance in many fields and of personality disorders. Google "big five personality" if you want an assessment of your personality.

predicted that equal rights for women would homogenize the genders now seem unfounded.

For those whose blood pressure has been raised by this framing of the nature/nurture debate, please note the following: First, personality differences between men and women are not caused only by genes. The current scientific consensus is that nature and nurture have roughly equal influences on behavioral tendencies that define personality.[83] Second, the 2008 study and its forebears are not arguing that efforts to achieve equality alone create greater personality differences, but that prosperity also plays a huge role – as will be explained shortly.[84] Fortunately, we live in a world in which progressive societies prosper and prosperous societies – excepting a few oil rich nations – are progressive.

The next question researchers sought to answer in the 2008 study was whether changes in men's personalities or women's most account for the greater gender differences found in progressive societies. For those readers with even an ounce of feminist sentiment, the urge to say women's might seem overwhelming, but the effect of prosperity is a clue to the correct answer. It turns out that modern cultures are mostly changing and benefiting men's personalities, not women's. One theory offered to explain this finding is that industrialization has increased the relative power of men and acted to enhance male personality traits – in part because the benefits of industrialization do not flow as much to women, who are more restrained by the responsibilities of child rearing.[85]

The researchers' alternative explanation is that the struggle just to survive in non-industrialized societies suppresses gender differences in personality. Where advances in civilization make life easier, innately influenced male personality traits such as assertiveness, dominance, risk taking and affinity for innovation blossom. It has been well documented that as progressive governments broaden opportunities, social class and other environmental advantages matter less in success and inherited traits matter more.[86] An analogous physical phenomenon is that there are greater differences in average height between men and women in more affluent cultures due to developmental "opportunities" afforded by better nutrition and medical care.[87] (But social progress is not uniformly advantageous for men. Gender differences in blood pressure, non-existent in some agrarian economies, are highest where modernity has liberated men's personalities to focus on career competition.[88])

The rise of more egalitarian societies and the decline of institutional and cultural barriers to opportunity are forces that eventually could equalize the opportunities each gender has for influence and wealth. But the resulting changes in men's personalities are creating new advantages for them that seem to be acting as a larger counterweight to whatever benefits for women accrue from the societal forces of equalization. To cite another of the researchers' analogies, in spite of laws equalizing opportunities in competitive track and field in the U.S., a far greater percentage of men cluster at the top – have times close to the best runners of their gender – than is the case for women.[89] Men are by their nature more competitive,[h] and greater opportunity seems to encourage their competitiveness more than women's.[90] As Harvard Law Professor Lani Guinier said, "it is not enough to just add women and stir."[91]

---

h. Brizendine at 22. Another example is Wikipedia, an online encyclopedia maintained by the public that is a reference source for most Internet users in the U.S. It encourages readers to correct the prior entries with more accurate information, and its competitive crowd sourcing engine seems to epitomize equal opportunity. A survey in 2010 found that women were only thirteen percent of its contributors. Cohen, Noam. But there is some evidence that gender differences in competitiveness may be narrowing. In 1992, a survey revealed that 80% of young men under 30 wanted a job with more responsibility, versus 72% of young women. By 2008, young men's zeal for promotion had waned considerably, with only two-thirds of both genders wanting that career bump. Galinsky at 1.

Two Jaws of the Paradox Trap

One of the paradoxes created when feminists insist that men and women are identical and should be identically treated is that sometimes they assert that women should get additional help in the areas where they are undeniably different from men. The issue of maternity leave split the women's movement in the 1970's, with some arguing that to ask for this would simply buy into the notion of gender differences that had been used since the beginning of time to deny women full participation in society.[i] The issue eventually was resolved by creating parental leave. In the health care debate in 2009-2010, there was controversy as to whether insurance should cover pregnancy, and if so whether women should pay more for health care than men. Manufactured identicalness does not resolve questions of fairness.

An even bigger problem is that by claiming sameness, feminists lose what could be their trump card in the quest to ensure women have equal access to influence and power: on average, women bring some different strengths to the table than men do. One example of difference that is easily described is violence.

---

i. A bank's challenge to a law permitting unpaid pregnancy leave for women because it discriminated against men polarized the feminist community. Groups such as the National Organization for Women and the National Women's Political Caucus supporting the bank's argument at the Supreme Court. Tavris at 117 (citing California Federal S. & L. Ass'n v. Guerra, 479 U.S. 272 (1987) (holding maternity leave law constitutional)).
In 2009, Italian women's groups opposed raising women's retirement age for government employees by five years to match that of men. Momigliano.

Propensity toward Violence

Women certainly are capable of violence. The first woman to be tried for war crimes in an international court, Pauline Nyiramasuhuko, made headlines for encouraging Hutu men to rape Tutsi women on an horrific scale in Rwanda.[92] No one will forget the heroism of Fort Hood SWAT Team Sergeant Kimberly Denise Munley, who on November 5, 2009 ran toward a deranged gunman and fired at him while he fired at her, causing him to run out of ammunition and ending his killing spree. She suffered five gunshot wounds.[93] And there has been much media attention on the growing number of women in criminal gangs or in prison.[94]

But violence is a part of only one of the three factors most responsible for the growth of female imprisonment: women are increasingly likely to be arrested during domestic violence incidents because state laws now require the arrest of anyone who inflicts even a slight injury. Violence does not explain the other two: women's progress in the workplace provides more opportunity to embezzle money, and greater numbers of women are abusing illegal drugs.[95]

On average, and of course we're talking about averages in these differences discussions, women do not come close to matching men's propensity for transforming aggression into violence.[96] In 1995, it was estimated that women constituted just ten percent of persons perpetrating violence against others,[97] a proportion that has changed little since then. Embezzlement, a nonviolent crime, is the only one women commit more often than men.[98] One study that looked at 700 years of murder records across a range of different cultures found male-on-male murders to be more than thirty times more numerous than female-on-female murders.[99] Robbery is *not* the main reason for that difference: studies show that two-thirds of murders committed by men stem from social conflicts.[100] Of those imprisoned for participating in the genocidal frenzy in Rwanda, just over two percent were women.[101]

Differences in the performance of male and female police officers illustrate the gender divide in propensity and attitudes toward violence. The San Jose, California Police Department tries to hire as many female officers as possible because studies show them to be more dependent on verbal skills to defuse trouble, and less reliant on force.[102] Although male and female officers perform their important responsibilities with equal proficiency, female officers typically are the subject of far fewer complaints of excessive use of force. Female officers cost the city less money in damage claim payments to victims of police violence.[103]

Levels of homicide vary from one nation to the next. Couldn't propensity to violence just be due to socialization and not innate tendencies? Environment could be a factor, but several innate gender differences created and maintained by evolution help drive men's greater propensity for violence. One is the predisposition toward taking risks involving injury or death, a factor in violence. Using violence often is risky. If you use force against someone, they or their kin may respond with violence against you. Why is the tendency to take such risks not the same for men and women? To explain that will require a quick primer or review – depending on the reader – of natural selection.

A Fishy Story with Legs

Charles Darwin is credited with first postulating how the various forms of life on earth came to be diverse. He defined the mechanism of natural selection: individuals with genetic mutations that cause advantageous physical traits or behaviors – especially in relation to changes to their environment such as climate, food supply, arrival of predators, etc. – are more likely to survive than those without such mutations. Thus they are more likely to pass their useful traits for survival down to subsequent generations. For both species and individuals, the measure of evolutionary success is the ability of a particular genetic line to proliferate over scores or thousands of generations by producing more offspring that successfully reproduce than competing lines. Scientists have explained creation of many traits in many species in this manner.[j] (The hottest scientific buzz as I write this is how rapid genetic changes enabled humans to speak.)

Natural selection also produces cultural evolution, based on the notion that groups within some species exhibit behavioral variations that are not solely the result of living in different environments. Individuals' advantageous behaviors spread within groups, with such behaviors of the preceding generation learned by the next. Less beneficial behaviors eventually die out because individuals in those groups that practice such behaviors have less reproductive success.[104] Zoologist Richard Dawkins has taken this a step further by using the principles of natural selection to describe how human cultural phenomena, what he calls *memes*, emerge, spread (reproduce) and sometimes extinguish.[105]

---

j. Some theorists explain seemingly useless traits as merely byproducts of other useful adaptations, or simply left over after environmental changes made them no longer necessary. Gould & Lewontin; Goode, *Human Nature*.

As far as I know I am unrelated to Darwin, despite the fact that his father was named Robert Waring Darwin.

Rejection of natural selection:	Considered by many to be the greatest scientist of all time, some rank Darwin the most influential person who's ever lived. Understanding evolution is absolutely essential to our being able to understand, treat and prevent the spread of rapidly evolving pathogens such as HIV, flu viruses and antibiotic resistant bacteria. Yet two hundred years after his birth there remains misunderstanding and skepticism about his ideas,[106] with the U.S. being the Western world's epicenter of popular disbelief of evolution. Even though mainstream science has accepted evolution as scientific fact for over forty years, teaching evolution in school is controversial in many states and it is common to hear that evolution is still just a theory or the work of Satan. The relentless efforts of religious conservatives to discredit Darwin's work as mere speculation have been so successful that the industry foes of policies responding to climate change have adopted similar tactics.

Nicolas Wade, a science writer, points out three ways in which people tend to reject Darwin's ideas. The first is through desire to see a purposeful intent in evolution,[107] both by some higher power and by individuals. But individuals have no control over the driving force of evolution: random genetic mutations that occur during procreation. Wade's second way stems from the first: doubt that evolution applies to human behavior,[108] in part because of a mistaken belief that unlike animals we are not driven by unconscious desires. Modern technology distorts the consequences of modern humans' unconscious drives, but we are still affected by these evolved desires even if they don't always seem rational in a modern context. Wade's third way is rejection of Darwin's notion that evolutionary forces act on groups – likely due to Western "people's tendency to think of themselves as individuals rather than as units of a group."[109]

Feminists vs. Darwin

Natural selection as first postulated was rather unfriendly to feminism, and even today some feminists have not laid to rest their antipathy for Darwin.[110] The problem with his story of how species evolved was that it largely left out females as key players. Early proponents of evolution, including Darwin, believed women evolved as mere reproduction machines, with limited intelligence or capacity for complex reasoning. They believed that because some robust men had scores of offspring, while lesser men had none, males' characteristics were the primary influence on the evolution of the human race.

Women, by contrast, could sequentially gestate only a limited number of offspring before menopause or death. The pregnancies of human hunter-gatherers (as well as those of bonobos and chimpanzees, our closest relatives) are widely spaced, with roughly five years separating siblings. Almost constant breast feeding stimulates hormone production that suppresses ovulation, and babies are not weaned until around age four. Female animals also mostly reproduced at the constant rate of their species.[111] (Darwin didn't know anything about DNA, but we'll see later that recent evidence supports his underlying assertion about gender differences in reproductive rates.)

But wait! In modern times there are many ways by which women alter their reproductive rate. More women are choosing not to procreate at all, while others seem bent on using fertility treatments to rival the legendary reproductive success of Genghis Khan. In 2009, one unemployed single mom in the U.S. made headlines by adding octuplets to her existing brood of six children.[112] Even long before the pill arrived, women were dramatically altering their birthrate. Most modern mothers – even in developing economies – supplement breast milk and often are engaged in tasks that reduce suckling below the level necessary to suppress ovulation. This can result in more children – more closely spaced.[113] The use of a wet nurse, although less common today, was another means by which new mothers quickly restored their fertility and raised their output of offspring.[114]

Unfortunately, the reproductive rate changes described in the preceding paragraph are too recent to refute Darwin and his contemporaries' sexist beliefs that women's relative lack of reproductive variability meant they had less effect on evolution and therefore were less "evolved" than men.[115] In the twentieth century, however, a greater understanding of evolution and the discovery of widespread evidence about the significant role females play in it debunked this notion of male superiority. It's safe for feminism to abandon its antipathy to evolutionary mechanisms and evolutionary psychology.[116]

Evolution has in many ways made females more important than males to the survival of many species, including humans. Looking at reproductive variability in another context reveals the proof: conditions can change the ratio of male to female offspring. If times get tough, a wide range of studies have found that there will be more female offspring in many species. When a mother's conditions for survival and reproduction are good, nature favors producing male offspring because a robust son can potentially produce a higher number of offspring of his own than can a daughter. When conditions are less favorable and less likely to produce robust offspring, shifts in a mother's hormones make daughters – a surer bet – more likely to result from mating. In hard times, a daughter has a greater probability than a son of at least producing some descendants.[117]

| *Want daughters? Skip breakfast.* | The slight decrease in the proportion of male births in industrialized countries since the 1950s has long puzzled demographers. Various explanations have been proposed and rejected, but one that has survived is based on – you guessed it – reproductive variability. A twenty-first century British study of first-time mothers' diets at the time of conception is one of many that find reproductive variability explains the phenomenon. With the women divided into three groups based on caloric intake, fifty-six percent of women in the highest calorie group bore boys, compared to forty-five percent in the lowest third. The study found no significant correlation to offspring gender in any of the other variables studied, including the mother's body mass index. |

The study's authors concluded that dietary changes may explain the percentage decline in male births and they highlight women's decision to skip breakfast. (Between 1965 and 1991 the percentage of U.S. adults eating breakfast fell from eighty-six to seventy-five percent, and declined from eighty-five to sixty-five percent for adolescent girls.) "Skipping breakfast extends the normal period of nocturnal fasting, depresses circulating glucose levels and may be interpreted by the body as indicative of poor environmental conditions."[118]

One of the most important concepts that came from Darwin's ideas applies to nearly all animals: female characteristics and behaviors that optimize the proliferation of females' genes compete with male characteristics and behaviors that favor males' genes.[119] In other words, each gender behaves in ways that maximizes its reproductive success. Each gender has some different needs and strategies for meeting them. We'll come back to this in the paradox about sex.

Motivation for Violence

Having finished our review of natural selection, we return to the issue of violence. One reason for the difference between men and women in their average propensity to take risks that could result in injury or death is reproductive variability. A man's exceptional success in life can provide him with access to many women who may bear him scores of offspring. Some ancient rulers had hundreds of children.[120] Modern genetic studies speculate that Genghis Khan, the 13th century Mongol emperor, could be the ancestor of sixteen million men, one out of every two hundred men alive today.[121] The extent of an individual's success frequently is a product of his skill and successful risk taking.

Natural selection often rewards those risk taking behaviors that can produce more offspring,[122] in spite of the chance that failure in economic competition or combat means that some men will have no descendants.[k]

Does DNA analysis show evidence of reproductive variability? Yes, the DNA inherited from fathers over hundreds of thousands of years is less variable than the DNA passed on by mothers. This means that compared to the number of women who became mothers, a smaller number of men successfully bred. On average each of these fathers produced a higher number of offspring than did women that reproduced.[l]

Another gender difference in the incentives toward risk taking is the time and resource investments each has in their offspring. A man's investment may be small – a single ejaculation. If he takes a risk that kills him after that, the mother often will ensure the child survives to adulthood. A woman gestates a child for nine months and a flood of bonding impulses when it is born compel her to nurse and nurture it for many more. If she takes a similar risk and dies, the child may die also – and that was especially true for our prehistoric human ancestors, when many of our inherent behavioral tendencies evolved. Women had greater disincentives to take risks than men did.

---

k. Some evolutionary theorists discount the notion that male promiscuity was the driving sexual force in human evolution and argue that other strategies such as monogamy offered as much chance for many males to maximize the propagation of their genes. Angier, *Men, Women, Sex and Darwin*; Barnett & Rivers, SAME DIFFERENCE at 61-69.

l. Pinker at 347. In a change too recent to affect evolution, this difference now has disappeared in modern industrialized societies. Equal numbers of men and women are procreating, and thus fathers and mothers are producing the same number of children on average. Fisher, THE FIRST SEX at 287. Increasing numbers of women are behaving like men and procreating with multiple partners.

Observations of the perilous behaviors of boys and men seem to bear out their greater propensity to take risks than girls and women, especially risks involving physical danger. New York City lags behind several other major U.S. cities in the ratio of women cyclists to men, says Transportation Professor John Pucher, primarily because the city has not done enough to make cycling there safer.[123] A mark of machismo in many cultures is willingness to risk injury or death, but I have never heard any woman express even the slightest interest in trying to outrun bulls for sport – as men come from all over the world to do annually in Pamplona, Spain. Men are significantly more attracted to some of my own sports of choice: male bastions such as paragliding and high altitude mountaineering. In nearly all human cultures that hunt large animals, men do nearly all of the hunting. And men comprise nearly all of the winners of the "Darwin Awards," a website that recounts peoples' foolhardy behaviors that take them out of the gene pool.[124]

Another gender difference driven by evolution is that females of many species, including humans and three of the four great apes, are often reproductively attracted to a male's violent aggression against other males. Such violence and victory demonstrate genetic fitness for procreation – that a bully and his mates' male offspring will more likely be endowed with characteristics that will give them successful progeny.[125] Violence also can make a female afraid not to mate with a bully, which explains why some female humans and chimpanzees stay with abusive partners.

Science has discovered some of the biochemical factors in aggression and violence. One is the hormone testosterone. Its level in the body rises before

and during aggressive and violent thoughts and behaviors. It naturally occurs at much higher levels in males than in females.[126] (With a few exceptions, such as the spotted hyena, and yes, in that species females are more aggressive than males.) Its effect on the blood, muscles and heart is one reason why top male athletes run, swim and bicycle faster than female athletes.[127] The brain of every human fetus starts out as female; if it has male genes, a flood of testosterone at the eighth week of gestation switches it to a male architecture with larger regions for aggression and sex.[128] But when fathers are involved in caring for their children they have lower levels of testosterone, a mechanism that presumably evolved to keep them focused on parenting.[129]

Testosterone also effects personality. Girls with lower in utero exposure to testosterone have a higher degree of sociability than girls with more exposure. In one study, four year old girls with less testosterone were the most popular playmates of either gender.[130] Another study showed that young women who are generally trusting are less so if given a dose of testosterone.[131] Yet another study found that a dose made college age women more egocentric and less collaborative.[132]

Spotted hyenas – girls gone wild:

Spotted hyenas of both genders have high levels of androgens (male sex hormones). This gives a female an enlarged clitoris that appears to be a penis and labia that look like a scrotum and testes.[133] (So it can be said these females have balls.) Newborns leave the womb swimming in these androgens, and come into the world with eyes open and a full set of sharp teeth. Normally twin siblings are born, and those of the same gender attack each other until one is dead.[134] Adult spotted hyenas are organized into mixed gender clans that females dominate and within which they fight for high rank. At least in female hyenas, it appears that high doses of male sex hormones can create a male appearance and aggressive behavior.

There is another unusual consequence of spotted hyenas' high level of male hormones – murder. Other than chimpanzees and humans, very few wild mammals kill adult members of their own species. The most prominent exceptions are wolves, lions, langur monkeys and spotted hyenas, which kill individuals they find near groups' territorial boundaries. (Unlike humans and chimpanzees, none of these species appear to engage in organized raiding against their own kind, although wolf packs and lion prides employ cooperative strategies in hunting prey.[135])

Oxytocin is often called the love drug.[m] Its levels rise in both

---

m. But it may not increase trust of outsiders. One experiment found male college students more likely to trust strangers after receiving a dose of oxytocin. Carey, *Hormone Dose* (citing Kosfeld). However, it was contradicted

genders during romance and it is believed to reinforce pair
bonding. Oxytocin is critical to the central nervous system's
effect on penis erection.[136] It also helps keep heart rate and
anxiety under control during stress.[137] Women naturally have
significantly higher levels of this hormone.[138]

Psychology Professor Shelley Taylor believes these hormones are
partly responsible for differences in how the genders tend to deal
with danger and extreme stress. Men are known for their fight or
flight response under stress, while women are more inclined to
"tend and befriend." Dr. Taylor has found that women typically
rely more on their social networks for protection and support,
probably also because women are less adapted for fighting, and
because they more often protect offspring and thus are unable to
easily flee.[139]

There also is evidence that an inherited gene, if combined with an
abusive upbringing, increases the likelihood of a child engaging
in violent and antisocial behavior later in life.[140] The gene in
question comes in two forms, a high producer of the calming
brain enzyme MAO-A that soaks up excess quantities of certain
neurotransmitters, and a low producer that is the cause of the
problem. Men have twice the risk of *not* inheriting at least one
copy of the beneficial high producer, because men have only one
copy of the gene whereas women have *two*.[141] (Although men and
women are very much alike, they share only ninety-eight percent
of their DNA – less than a human shares with a chimpanzee or
bonobo of the same gender.)

War, and the killing that accompanies it, is male violence
organized on a mass scale. It brings risks but also gains to tribes

---

by other experiments on men in which a dose promoted more favorable
attitudes and cooperative economic behavior toward members of subjects'
affinity group, but caused no changes toward those outside their group. De
Dreu.

or societies that perpetrate it. One natural selection mechanism that encouraged war was that it enabled male warriors to spread their genes to more females in vanquished societies, and reduced the likelihood that vanquished males could impregnate females in the victor's society – more of the Genghis Khan effect. Recognizing that in a majority of human cultures women migrate for marriage while men do not,[142] the roots of war also can be understood as coercive importation of fertile women. By stealing and subjugating desirable women, tribes of successful warriors may have gotten better female genes than they otherwise would have from peaceful migration. Raiding foes' villages and abducting their fertile women occurred as far back in history as warfare itself.[143] Studies of remote tribes that still engage in raids have found that stealing fertile women remains an important motive for warfare.[144]

The paradox of war:	The fact that some forms of organized violence are not rational in modern times, yet still persist, gives credence to the notion that such violence is deeply ingrained in human – especially men's – behavior. A study that illustrates this phenomenon asked the question: if you were the leader of nation, would you rather face a nonviolent rebellion or one that employs violent resistance? If you answered nonviolent, the results of a study of 323 national resistance movements from 1900 to 2006 may surprise you. Only a quarter of violent campaigns prevailed, in large part because violent resistance gives a regime the excuse to respond with force. By contrast, more than half of nonviolent campaigns achieved success. Using only nonviolent resistance gives a regime little justification to respond with violence, and diminishes both domestic and international support for the regime if it does.[145] Thus, violently resisting an oppressive regime usually is an irrational choice given that the odds of success are less than half of those for nonviolent campaigns. That violent resistance movements are not rare despite their ineffectiveness, and that all are led by men, is testament to men's strong tendency to resort to violence.

None of the preceding should be interpreted to mean that there is a stark divide on attitudes toward war, with women opposing war and men supporting it. Nor does it mean that a woman in leadership position would not advocate for war –Margaret Thatcher and Condoleezza Rice belie that notion. But it does help explain why women and men on average feel differently about when war is necessary. Polls show more women than men back international police actions to stop ongoing genocide.[146] In America after 9/11, women and men in equal numbers overwhelmingly favored invading Afghanistan – the nation that harbored the murderous terrorists and where women were suffering and dying because of their gender.[147] This was significantly different from the first and second Gulf Wars – supported by about two-thirds of American men, but only half of American women.[148]

Proponents of sameness tout violence:	In their book *Same Difference*, Rosalind Barnett and Caryl Rivers attempt to knock down the idea that men and women are different. Using anecdotes about women's increasing use of violence, they attempt to persuade the reader that women's aggression can translate into violence just as readily as men's. They use a chart to emphasize the results of a *video game* study published in 1994 showing that when participants' anonymity was assured, women dropped more bombs on their opponents than men did.[149] But using such a study of college students to infer that women are inherently just as prone to actual violence as men is ludicrous. If this study truly proved the proposition that both genders are equally prone to violence, there would have been other studies since 1994 bolstering this conclusion. But Barnett and Rivers offer none. (There's another example from their book discussed in the Appendix.)

To further support their assertion about female violence, Barnett and Rivers tout the fact that three of the first seven soldiers charged in the Abu Ghraib prison scandal were women.[150] But, they ignore the pressure these women faced to fit in with their male peers. They don't mention that clerk Lynndie England, the most photographed of the three women, was psychologically controlled by the father of her child, the guards' ringleader Charles Graner. As later investigation revealed, abuse of military prisoners became *de rigueur* after 9/11, and was encouraged by men at the highest levels of government

Paradox Revisited

Eliminating cultures' assignment of gender roles is a worthy goal, but not because of feminism's expectation that gender sameness likely will emerge. Rather, a greater range of working styles and perspectives could increase productivity and improve policy making. Women's particular perceptions, analyses, ideations, connections and actions are not always the same as men's. Women's decision making strategies and choices could be different from those of the men historically and currently in power. True, there is some risk of rekindling discrimination by highlighting differences between men and women, but the greater risk is in failing to fully utilize some of these differences.

Reaping previously untapped benefits from gender differences will require dealing with the other bombshell found in the 2008 personality study and discussed in the next paradox.

Challenges in predicting the effects of gender differences:

It's hard to resist the temptation to predict how the world would improve if more women were in charge. Women generally are more empathetic and cooperative, and are better communicators than men. Wouldn't they carry these values into their leadership? The problem is that the expression of some of the tendencies of each gender is influenced by circumstances. Women will often behave like men if they are rewarded for doing so, and vice versa. A society's choice of values may be more important than its choice of particular leaders.

A meta study of doctors published in 2002 illustrates the difficulties of such predictions. The data clearly shows that women doctors spend more time with patients, engage in more emotionally focused conversation and are more likely to treat the relationship as a partnership – except in the specialty of obstetrics and gynecology. There, male physicians engage in more psychosocial discussion than their female counterparts. One theory offered to explain this disparity is that Ob/gyn patients strongly prefer female doctors, unlike in all other areas of medicine where patients of both genders have historically preferred male physicians. A subgroup of practitioners in any trade will work harder to connect with clients if they are trying to gain acceptance.[151] (But unlike in this case, motivating one gender to behave more like the other does not always lead to the adoption of positive values.)

Paradox 3: Feminism Has Not Made Women Happier.

Regardless of how one answers the question of whether there are differences between men and women that are not the product of historical oppression, which the second paradox examined, a key question is whether women are happier – absolutely or relative to men – if they have greater social equality and career opportunities. The goals of feminism have been asserted on the premise that once women were liberated from patriarchy and able to have equal bargaining power in relationships, chose their own paths and pursue their individual potential, women would be happier and more fulfilled. Now that many of the granddaughters of the second-wave feminists of the late 1960's and early 70's are themselves working, mothers, or both, it seems both fair and prudent to assess whether that premise was in fact predictive, or whether happiness paradoxically remains upside down.

Let's look at another study – this one finding that it's women who are experiencing most of the changes, but not in a good way. Its title describes its conclusions: *The Paradox of Declining Female Happiness*.[152] Based on long term, widespread data, it found that "women's happiness has fallen both absolutely and relative to men's" across much of the industrialized world from the mid 1970's through the first decade of the twenty-first century.[153] This decline is true regardless of women's employment or marital status, age, level of education or whether they have children.[154] (However, having more education does correlate with greater unhappiness.) European women fared a little better; with satisfaction having increased for both genders, but women's happiness relative to men declining.[155] The authors ask the obvious question: "Did men garner a disproportionate share of the benefits of the women's movement?" At least one self-help book about women's happiness based on the study – *Find Your Strongest Life* – agrees that men have fared better.[156]

It's tempting to think that this paradoxical result is due to women working more total hours now that wage earning work has been added to housework. But that explanation is not supported by the evidence, say *The Paradox* authors. They cite another study documenting nearly equal relative declines in total work hours for both men and women in the forty years since 1965, with growth in women's workplace hours more than offset by big reductions in the time spent maintaining home and family. Similarly, men now are working fewer hours in the workplace with some of that loss made up by more hours spent on family responsibilities. (However, women still have primary physical and emotional responsibility for home and family.) Yet another forty-year study found that with their new mix, women's pleasure in their day has stayed the same. Men, by contrast, have had a net increase in the pleasantness of activities in their day.[157] Time spent on the average job may not be as much fun as time spent with the average family.

There are two theories for the unhappiness paradox that the authors say their research neither supports nor refutes. The first is that with greater equality, more women are comparing their life circumstances to those of the men around them instead what they used to do – compare themselves only to other women. Since men remain dominant and better off in many ways, logically this would leave women feeling in a relatively lower position than when their point of reference was only other women. Or maybe, so the second theory goes, it's that the women's movement fueled high expectations that have proved impossible for most women to attain, leaving most disappointed by the lives they've actually led.[158] This would help explain why most women feel alienated from feminism.

A third unhappiness theory they provide is that women have taken on the stress of new financial responsibilities. One way of understanding this starts with an old wedding rehearsal dinner joke: "A woman worries about the future until she gets a husband. A man never worries about the future until he gets a wife." Many women now shoulder a substantial burden in providing for their financial future and that of their families. In this view, women's unhappiness is mostly the result of women taking on this traditionally male burden and being underprepared for that responsibility. This theory is borne out by the data. Women's satisfaction with their financial circumstances has moved steadily downward since the mid 1970's, and by 2007 women were "substantially less satisfied with their household financial situation" than were men.[159]

Addressing these first two theories, one might respond that the decline in women's happiness should resolve as women gain a better ability to set realistic life path expectations for themselves. But why should women have to be "realistic" about fitting into career expectations in a work world they had little part in creating? Isn't it understandable that women would feel less satisfied in a world where their likely earnings and career trajectories will by design fall short of those of men? Why should women, or for that matter, humankind, accept the status quo? As feminist icon Gloria Steinem asked, "If the shoe doesn't fit, must we change the foot?"

Addressing the third theory, perhaps women will get used to worrying more about their financial futures. But when your earnings potential is nearly always less than that of a similarly situated man (as described in paradox one), your worry is likely to be greater.

Neurotic Inertia

The 2008 personality study across fifty-five cultures described in the second paradox found that men's personalities are changing in more progressive and prosperous cultures. Perhaps the biggest bombshell in this study is that prosperity seems to making men less moody, irritable, stressed, hysterical or depressed. Psychologists' shorthand for this is less neurotic.[160] If not feeling in control – a mental state very common in less prosperous nations – is making a person neurotic, then feeling more in control should lessen those symptoms. It is not surprising that as the progressive values of prosperous societies have increased personal and financial autonomy, men are seeing the most benefit from this, while women are not benefiting as much. Men are less tied to child rearing obligations than women, and more rewarded by societal success standards and professional achievement criteria set by men. With prosperity reducing men's neuroticism, other inherently influenced personality traits such as the need for domination and risk taking are more effectively able to express themselves. In industrialized economies, men's stress seems to be channeled into increased blood pressure.[161]

If women are seeing any reduction in their level of neuroticism from cultural progress, this is not showing up in personality surveys. Any dips probably are being negated by greater stress from new challenges bought on by that progress. For an increasing number of women in progressive societies, prosperity comes with increased demands. Women often have to be super mom, super wife, and a professional success all at the same time, as well as worry about their families' financial security far more than when most women were housewives. It's no wonder many women say they can never do enough to feel in control of their lives. In short, because life is disproportionately better for men in prosperous nations, women are being left behind.

Some neurotic labels that seem anti-feminist persist:	Perhaps the neurosis most associated with women is hysteria. This disorder helped cause the Salem witch trials,[162] was popularized two centuries later by Sigmund Freud and others,[163] and led to the invention of the vibrator.[164] While many feminists have asserted that hysteria is just a patriarchal label intended to further marginalize women,[165] it does not seem to be disappearing, even in societies where women have made great progress toward equality with men.[166]

Work/Life Imbalance

Professor Anne-Marie Slaughter posited a fourth theory about women's unhappiness beyond those offered by the *The Paradox* authors. For many cultural and innate reasons women may be less happy, because on average they have stronger needs than men to care for their children – or parents or other infirm family members – and more guilt when they do not.[167] The life multitasking that stresses women often is called work/life balance. But for many women it's best described as an imbalance. For example, some women at home full time would rather be in the workplace, but full time means a grueling work schedule that's hell on them and their families. There are few fulfilling part time opportunities in their professions. These women want interesting and challenging jobs with humane schedules that don't exist.

The percentage of employers offering flextime, part time or job sharing *dropped significantly* between 2001 and 2004, according to a survey by the Society for Human Resource Management.[168] The layoffs and high unemployment of 2008's Great Recession not only stopped the overall growth of work/life programs, mostly viewed by employers as tools for retention, but also greatly reduced fearful employees' use of such programs.[169] (While work/life usually is seen as a women's issue, many male employees care about work/life also – just not to the extent that women do.)

In 2010, celebrating the fiftieth anniversary of the pill in a *New York Times* op-ed, Professor Elaine Tyler May declared, "Today, women no longer need to choose between having a family and a career."[170] But for some professional women, it is nearly impossible to meet the expectations of their employers and the demands of motherhood simultaneously. In the 2007 book *Opting Out?: Why Women Really Quit Careers and Head Home*, Sociology Professor Pamela Stone concluded that many successful professional women who become mothers quit their jobs only as a last resort rather than as a choice to spend full time with their children. The more than fifty professionals she interviewed "found themselves marginalized and stigmatized, negatively reinforced for trying to hold onto their careers after becoming mothers."[171]

The National Academy of Sciences published a report in 2006 in response to controversial comments by Harvard President Larry Summers about women's low representation on math, science and engineering faculties. The report, entitled *Beyond Bias and Barriers: Fulfilling the Potential of Women in Academic Science and Engineering*, states that women in science face discrimination in workplace attitudes and policies toward balancing work and family responsibilities. The report argued that unless universities reform their practices, the nation will continue to be deprived of women's talents.

In 2009, the self help book *Womenomics* offered advice for women looking to reduce the hours of their full time jobs or create flexible schedules.[172] But such desires may still be impractical in an economy with high unemployment, reduced bargaining power for employees, and workplaces where old values often remain entrenched. Many corporations cling to the views of leaders such as the legendary ex-CEO of GE, Jack Welch, considered by some to be one of the greatest business leaders of all time. Welch said in 2009, "There's no such thing as work-life balance." Instead, he insisted, there are work/life choices – with consequences for each choice, such as slower career advancement and reduced chances for reaching the top.[173] In dismissing a class action lawsuit in 2011 alleging discrimination against new mothers by Bloomberg L.P., a financial information and technology company, Federal Judge Loretta Preska quoted Welch and also declared, "The law does not mandate 'work-life balance.' "[174]

A 2007 survey of female MBA's from the University of Chicago's School of Business bears this out. Of those graduating since 1990, only half of the women out ten or more years that had children still were working full time.[175] Reviewing studies of women with Harvard undergraduate degrees, the survey authors also found that it is harder for MBAs to combine "career and family" than for physicians, PhDs, and attorneys.[176]

But try telling that to a female lawyer. In the legal profession part time or post-birth work still remains largely incompatible with career advancement, and the kinds of assignments given to part time workers or new mothers often are not professionally satisfying.[177] A 2001 report by Deborah Rhode found that "95 percent of law firms now have policies allowing part-time work," but "only three percent of lawyers actually work part time."[178] As one lawyer and mother said, "The chances for a woman to make partner at my firm are slim, and motherhood takes you completely off partner-track."[179] While some large firms have offered part time partner tracks in recent years, the overall effect on women has been offset by the increasingly longer hours demanded of associates and partners, especially as the Great Recession spawned massive layoffs and froze new hiring. The percentage of women lawyers in the largest two-hundred and fifty U.S. law firms declined between 2006 and 2010.

Many women don't even attempt to have a family in this environment. Whether career pressure not to procreate is a source of unhappiness is unclear – various surveys find that people without children are generally happier than those with,[180] while others find no difference.[181] But it is often true that when which side of the fence you are on does not feel like your choice, the grass seems greener on the other side. There is a conflict in America between motherhood and a professional career reflected in the fact that at the turn of the century, eighty-one percent of forty year old men with six figure incomes had children, while among women only fifty-one percent with those same attributes had procreated.[182] In academia, only thirty-eight percent of women with tenure in the humanities and social sciences had children by the time they were forty – an average of thirteen years after earning their doctorates.[183] The headline of a 2006 article in *Forbes Magazine* warned male professionals interested in starting families: "Don't Marry Career Women."[184]

The women that take a few years off for their families may face limited opportunities to reenter their careers. As Sylvia Ann Hewlett, author of *Creating a Life*, describes it, there are many off ramps, but few on ramps.[185] A *Newsweek* cover story in 2006 attempted to highlight the progress that various firms were making in creating on ramps for female professionals. The few featured examples were disheartening. The investment firm Lehman Brothers in 2005 started a biannual seminar program for mothers wanting to return to Wall Street called "Encore." The firm of 23,000 employees had hired a grand total of sixteen women via this program as of September 2006.[186] The economic free fall in 2008 largely ended such opportunities in the investment industry when Lehman Brothers and other large firms collapsed in ruin or were acquired.

Consulting firm Booz Allen Hamilton allowed over one hundred women who had off-ramped to take discrete projects on a contract basis in 2006 – with no health benefits. The firm said the purpose of the program is to encourage these contractors, called "adjuncts," to come back – when they were ready to resume the grueling, more than full time schedule they had left earlier in order to have time for their families. If Booz Allen was interested in hiring these women back as employees with less than full time schedules, they didn't tell *Newsweek*.[187] The gender discrimination lawsuit filed in 2010 by former Goldman Sachs Vice President Charlotte Hanna, demoted after she took a part time track and then laid off while on her second maternity leave, opened a debate about whether the suit would create opportunities for mothers or instead discourage firms from hiring women or offering part time work.[188]

One off-ramped attorney wrote a book of advice to returning moms. Her main suggestion? List your former job title on forms filled out for children's schools and doctors – so as to maintain your professional identity.[189] Because expected improvements in progress for women failed to materialize after the last "bursts of enthusiasm for on-site day care or job sharing," the *Newsweek* article conceded that corporate focus on on ramps may be just another fad.[190] Whether fad or not, no one has any ideas how women can replace the income and future earning power lost when they stay at home for a few years. Sylvia Hewlett estimates the future income lost is ten percent of salary for every two years away, a penalty that rarely ever disappears.[191]

In middle and low income households, just as for professional women, few mothers who stay home with their children do so by choice, a 2008 Congressional study reported. The study concluded that because employment rates for mothers are not significantly lower than they are for all women, most of the mothers that left the workforce after 2001 to stay at home did so because of an economic downturn,[192] or for some other involuntary reason. In many lower skilled jobs with no sick leave, women who stay home to care for sick children are terminated. Women also may stay home because they lack affordable childcare. Nowhere is this more crucial than for women trying to improve their employability by obtaining a college degree. Yet between 2001 and 2008, the percentage of community colleges offering child care fell to less than fifty percent.[193]

Yet another factor discouraging mothers' participation in the workforce is commonly called the marriage tax. In the U.S., the income of a spouse is taxed at a higher rate than that of the family's so-called first earner. A few progressive nations such as Sweden and Switzerland don't have a marriage tax. By contrast, in 2007 Spain and Italy were taxing second income at a rate sixty percent higher than the income of the first earner.[194] If you are married and use tax preparation software for your taxes, try this test: Create two single returns from copies of your joint return and delete the other spouse's W-2's, 1099's and deductions from each single return. Then add the two tax bills each spouse would have had if single, subtract that sum from the tax owed on the joint return and prepare for a shock. The difference is the tax penalty on working spouses. The message seems to be: wives should not work, so we'll discourage it by taxing their income at a higher rate than their husbands'. My wife and I paid over ten percent more on our 2008 taxes than we would have if we were single and cohabiting. (While some other economic benefits exclusively due to marriage may partially offset the tax, most of those are retirement related and decades away for most taxpayers.[195])

Ironically, even though some societies seem to be sending the message to young women that they should forego careers and stay home to have babies, that's not what they're doing. Couples appear to be deciding that without that second income, they can't afford to have children. Comparisons of national fertility rates according to the gap between men and women's employment show that countries with more equal employment have the highest fertility rates. Not coincidentally, most of those countries have affordable, quality childcare and don't tax second incomes at a higher rate.[196]

Part of the long term challenge in attaining greater universal happiness is that women are different than men and different things make them happy or unhappy. Simply ensuring that women have all the things that men have may not make them as happy as men. Maybe they need some things that men don't need, or perhaps some things that make men happy actually make women unhappy. Feminism's happiness goal was never supported by a viable implementation strategy. Such a strategy could have asserted that making twenty-first century women happy would lead us to create new social, political and economic structures that would build a better and happier society for us all. To do that you have to convince the public that fulfilling the genders' needs is not a zero sum game – and that there are ways to make women happier without decreasing men's happiness, as some European nations have proved over the past several decades.[197] More about this in chapter twelve.

Paradox 4: Women Still Are Less Able to Ask for What They Want.

Feminism intended to empower women to advocate for themselves, and to remove cultural political and economic barriers that have stood in their way. But this goal has proved to be more elusive than originally hoped. Due to the attitudes of both men and women, our society is far from gender equality in opportunity. It's a paradox that despite an arc of outspoken icons that includes the Virginia Slims liberated woman with skinny cigarettes, Thelma and Louise, and Sarah Palin, women who are assertive to men in the workplace still risk social disapproval.

There have been numerous news reports that women are not as assertive as men in negotiating starting salaries and raises.[198] Women are much less likely to ask for a promotion and more inclined to say they are not ready if one is offered.[199] Linda Babcock and Sara Laschever's book, *Women Don't Ask*, cites a study showing that only seven percent of the women in one masters degree program negotiated the salary of their first job, whereas fifty-seven percent of the men in the same program did. Extrapolating those higher starting salaries to increased salaries in subsequent years created an estimated one million dollar difference in individual lifetime earnings between these men and women.[200]

You might read these startling statistics and think that women just need motivational training. They should get tough and demand what is rightfully theirs! But that would not set things right. Women appear to accurately perceive the strong and unique disincentive female workers have to negotiate with male superiors. Study after study shows that if a woman tries to negotiate a starting salary, a male doing the hiring is likely to be much less interested in hiring her.[201] Such bias is not easy to eliminate.

Women also may believe that appearing too confident in other ways may subject them to bias. A 2009 study of 250 male and female managers across a range of industries found that women managers underestimated how their superiors would rate their performance (using nine comprehensive criteria) three times as often as male managers. Professor Scott Taylor observed that while women "have imposed their own glass ceiling," the men in the study overestimated how they would be rated.[202] The fact that the study found the discrepancy to be less for women younger than fifty suggests that the confidence and assertiveness gap may decrease in a generation or two as older women leave the workforce and younger women replace them.

But women may still enter the male dominated culture of business, built on overselling one's self, coming from societal norms that encourage girls and women to be more self-effacing.[203] In a European report on gender prepared by McKinsey & Company in 2007, a bank board member said, "On the same project, men will demonstrate 100% ambition even if they only have 50% of the required skills, whereas the women will be concerned about having only 80% of the required skills."[204] There remains a wide confidence gap even in Norway, known for its advancements in gender egalitarianism. A female Danish economist who led Norway's main business lobby's effort to recruit women into upper management said in 2010, "I don't think I've ever heard a female oversell her capabilities."[205]

Perhaps in the future assertiveness will become less important to success in the workplace. But that proposition is a tough sell. Or maybe time will bring a significant change in women's assertiveness in the workplace. However, with no agreed upon ways to increase assertive qualities in women, no agreed upon targets, and a national Zeitgeist that gender inequalities no longer need to be remedied, such change seems unlikely.

Paradox 5: Women Still Discriminate against Women.

Feminism preached that the biggest obstacle to women's advancement was men who did not want to share power and influence.[206] The movement sought to overcome male resistance to women's progress. Women ultimately would prevail in this contest, so it was thought, partly by demonstrating competence in skills formerly thought to be within the exclusive domain of men.

First the good news: although the jury is still out as to whether women make better business managers than men, in the aggregate there is promising data. A study by Catalyst found substantially higher returns on equity in American companies with more women in senior management positions as compared to companies with fewer women leaders.[207] Another study found that among the companies in France's major share price index (CAC 40), a company's share price fell less in 2008 (start of the Great Recession) the more women there were in its management.[208] But it's hard to know whether this data reflects superiority in women's aptitude for management or just shows that only the best women manage to punch through a glass ceiling. The latter may be what is happening in France. A 2010 survey found that while nearly everyone in France supported equal rights for women, more than eighty percent believed that "men still got more opportunities than women for jobs that pay well, even when woman were as qualified."[n]

Why Can't Women Just Get Along?

The bad news is that discrimination against women does not just come from men. In fact, women may face harassment from women just as much or more as from men. In the U.S. and some other nations with modern economies, an impediment to women's progress is that many women still question the competence of female professionals and prefer to be treated by male doctors (except in OB/GYN), represented by male lawyers, and taught by male teachers.[209] Perhaps the greatest challenge is that faced by female managers. When I worked for IBM in the late 1970s, it was the women in my office of one hundred employees who most complained about the only female manager who worked there. Why is it still true that many women believe that women in traditionally male roles are less able than men?

A significant number of women in the workplace say they prefer to work with and for men rather than women, and complain that women are more apt than men to be threatened by well performing female coworkers or subordinates, be combative over unimportant details, and hold petty grudges.[210] A 2005 study of a thousand American workers in various industries examined mental and physical stress. Men did better where they had access to the managerial skills of both genders – where they shared a male and female supervisor. Women had fewer stress related ailments and concentration problems while working exclusively for men, and were worst off working only for women. The

---

n. Shannon. Of twenty-two countries polled across five continents, France had the highest percentage of people – seventy-five percent – that believed men have a better life than women. Bennhold, *Where Having It All*. Professor Herminia Ibarra, co-author of the World Economic Forum's *2010 Corporate Gender Gap Report* notes that French "business culture remains resolutely a boys' club." Shannon.

findings were consistent, with a few exceptions, across a range of occupations, industry sectors, and work-related variables.[211]

Why might this be? One theory is that for many women, their relationships with men are the most important determinant of their social, political and economic status.[212] As the subordinate class, women still compete for a narrow range of opportunities according to rules set by dominant men.[213] Because men are still mostly in charge, women are more likely to obtain success in business and government from loyalty to those men and to male values. Some women's loyalties toward their male patrons are at the expense of their bonds with other women they regard as competitors for that patronage.[214]

This influence is so powerful that some women who do make it to the top do not want to call attention to their gender, and do not appear interested in helping other women climb the ladder.[215] In one study women psychology professors had the same gender biases as men, and preferred to hire men as new professors.[216] At law firms, a lack of interest by women partners in mentoring women associates is cited as a key reason why women leave law firms at nearly twice the rate of men.[217] The focus of high achieving women often is on fitting into a male world and surviving the rigors of high altitude. This seems especially true for CEOs, a position held by women in less than two percent of Fortune 500 companies at the end of 2006. "Nearly all" of the nine female CEOs a *New York Times* reporter contacted in 2006 were unwilling to comment for an article about female CEOs.[218]

Social Males

What some say is happening when women compete in the workplace is that they emulate men, but not necessarily by choice. In order to compete with men at work, many women report surrendering some of their female identity. Success may require behaving like a man, while behaving like a woman may be an obstacle to success. As one feminist observed, "To the extent that women cannot or will not conform to socially male forms of behavior, they are left out in the cold. To the extent they do or can conform, they do not achieve equality as *women*, but as social males."[219]

The legal profession is a useful window through which to view these social phenomena. Lamenting the loss of gender identity, some women lawyers complain that their female "voices were 'stolen' from them during the first year" of law school.[220] Their professors and employers tell them that "learning to think like a lawyer means learning to think and act like a man."[221] Logic should replace emotions, and compassion is inappropriate.[222] A female law student reflected, "[F]or me the damage is done; *it's in me.* I will never be the same. I feel so defeated."[223] According to Law Professor Lani Guinier, American legal education's model is:

> a lawyer who uses rights-based reasoning to analyze legal problems in terms of competing, mutually exclusive claims. He can argue all sides of any issue, because he has no personal stake in any of his arguments. In form, the model lawyer also demonstrates characteristics traditionally associated with maleness: aggression, willingness to fight, emotional detachment, and exaggerated bravado. Women who learn that lawyering equals maleness may be stifled in their ability to form a whole, integrated professional identity.... For all practical purposes, many women students are faced with the choice of trading their identities as women for identities as lawyers.[224]

It's like a science fiction movie where the conquerors take over the minds of those in the dominated population, turning them into alien agents. For one student, the beginning of the process felt like being violated in the classroom: "When I get called on, I really think about rape. It's sudden. You're exposed. You can't move. You can't say no. And there's this man who's in control, telling you exactly what to do."[225] Women in Guinier's study of legal education reported more mental health distress than did their male counterparts.°

Women face this risk in any job or career in which men make the rules – pretty close to every job in the workplace. As *New York Times* columnist Nicholas Kristof said, "There's a risk that we make the mistake of thinking that the basic problem is just men. ... The problem is patriarchal attitudes that are absorbed and transmitted by women almost as much as by men."[226] And we often fail to appreciate the completeness of women's transformation. For example, you would not expect a woman to lead the fight against legislation to help women receive wages equal to those of men performing the same work. But who was the author of the Senate amendment that unsuccessfully attempted to nullify the Lilly Ledbetter Fair Pay Act of 2009? It was the senior Republican woman in the Senate, Kay Bailey Hutchison, also an unsuccessful candidate for Governor of Texas in 2010. (Perhaps in a face saving effort, in the final tally she did vote for the Act, which corrects a Supreme Court ruling that made it very difficult for many women to bring discrimination lawsuits based on unequal pay.)

But is competition among women any more of a problem for women's advancement than competition among members of any subordinate group striving for equality? Just as described above, members of some minority groups hold professionals in the dominant majority group in higher esteem because they believe

---

o. Guinier at 44. While this dispassionate approach disproportionately disturbs women, it also saddens some male students. I'll never forget the dismay I felt when Supreme Court Justice Antonin Scalia told me that "compassion has no place in the law."

they are more skilled or influential than members of their own group. Once some individual members of minority groups succeed in the dominant culture, they pull the ladder up and refuse to help others like themselves follow in their path. And some members of minority cultures who try to achieve in the dominant society complain that this requires surrendering their cultural identities and accepting the dominant paradigm.

All true, but one of the things that makes competition among women in a man's world different is that it has parallels in sexual competition for mates. Some of that competition is hardwired in our behavior because its roots go back tens, if not hundreds, of millions of years. Ethnic competition within communities has a far more recent history and perhaps a less primal influence on behavior. Also, the genetic competition between the genders described in paradox two may be at the root of the following gender difference that can be especially powerful in the workplace.

Relational Aggression

The explanation for why some women make other women uncomfortable in the workplace may be more than just that some have succumbed to a workplace version of Stockholm syndrome.[p] When women compete with other women, they can be uniquely more effective than men because they honed these skills in middle school. Feminist historian Elizabeth Fox-Genovese observed that "those who have experienced dismissal by the junior-high-school girls' clique could hardly, with a straight face, claim generosity and nurture as a natural attribute of women."[227] A spate of books in 2002 described high levels of the "relational aggression" in middle-school-aged girls who cruelly gossip about

---

p. A syndrom in which a victim gradually identifies with those who are controlling her.

and socially ostracize their peers.[228] Girls devise various social competitions aimed at ranking each other according to popularity. They suddenly can become astonishingly cruel to both their enemies and friends, especially toward those who lag behind in popularity or are less able to socially defend themselves.

Sadly, there may be a worsening trend in this behavior. 2010 saw increasing reports of girls in kindergarten and early elementary school grades fiercely bullying less "mature" peers. Some attribute this meanness to parents and popular culture encouraging girls to believe that their popularity depends on how much their social aggression and style of dressing makes them seem older than their peers.[229]

At all ages, women and girls possess social skills that ironically make them particularly destructive as social competitors:

- Women understand and can "manage" relationships. As Finnish researcher Kaj Bjorkqvist concluded, girls' "superior *social* intelligence enabled them to wage complicated battles with other girls aimed at damaging relationships or reputations."[230]

- Women have strong *empathic* abilities. "Girls can better understand how other girls feel," as Bjorkqvist observed, "so they know better how to harm them."[231] Psychology Professor Marion Underwood notes, "Girls very much value intimacy, which makes them excellent friends and terrible enemies. They share so much information when they are friends that they never run out of ammunition if they turn on one another."[232]

Misplaced Benevolence?

Not convinced of the competition theory? How about that in not lending a hand, women are simply trying in some upside down way to be benevolent toward other women? Perhaps they believe that other women coming up in the world will face discrimination and want to spare them the heartache of reaching for goals they likely cannot achieve, or toughen them up to try harder. If thinking that's still the way things are in the U.S. in the twenty-first century makes your head hurt, it may get worse – because that's the conclusion of a well designed study of gender's influence on assessments of professional competence.[233]

In 2008, a researcher randomly sent script excerpts written by four established women playwrights to theater companies in the United States and asked for their feedback in a survey.[234] Half the scripts were identified as having been written by playwrights with female pseudonyms and half with male pseudonyms. Eighty-two theater artistic directors or literary managers responded, about half of those that could have. Half of the responders were men and half were women.[235]

The survey results clearly showed that scripts evaluators believed were written by women faced discrimination. The source of the discrimination – get out the aspirin – came entirely from the female evaluators and not from the males. Female evaluators gave scripts they thought women had written lower ratings for likable characters, audience appeal, economic viability, likelihood of being produced and chances of winning a prize. But it wasn't that the evaluators liked those scripts any less than the others. When the survey asked about "artistic exceptionalism" and whether evaluators would produce the play, differences by gender disappeared.[236]

The author of the survey, with help from some top shelf academics, laid the blame on a widespread belief that the works of women playwrights are riskier investments than those of men. A factor behind the discrimination is a theater's perceived risk in investing in a new playwright. In this view, women may have less likelihood of a successful career due to taking time off to have a family, or from raw discrimination by other theaters and producers.[237]

Women's scripts have to be better:	If female artistic directors and literary managers believe that women playwrights face a harsher world than men, their harsher ratings of women's scripts would certainly create a self-fulfilling prophesy by being an additional barrier for women. But is there evidence of discrimination against women playwrights – beyond what they face from female script evaluators – that may help explain the misplaced "benevolence" phenomenon? To figure it out, the researcher looked at the average revenue from Broadway productions written by women versus those written by men. Women's revenues were higher – and there was no evidence their production costs were higher – but shows based on their scripts did not run any longer than those of men. Assuming producers make rational profit decisions, it would have made sense to have run more profitable productions longer. But that was not the case. Even though greater ticket sales indicated women's scripts were better, that did not inspire the confidence of producers.

> The higher revenues demonstrated one more aspect of discrimination: women face a higher barrier to entry. Because ticket sales show their scripts are more popular then men's, it's clear that women's scripts on average have to be better than men's in order to get produced.[238] Or flipped around, men's scripts don't have to be as good. Perhaps it's because more male playwrights have established connections in the theater that work in their favor.
>
> A 1997 study showed gender discrimination in the assessment of academic writing where experience was equal. Women applicants for post-doctoral positions "either had to publish at least three more papers in a prestigious science journal or an additional 20 papers in lesser-known specialty journals" to be ranked as high as men.[239]

One additional finding makes the discrimination by women seem both more deeply entrenched, and more disturbing. Plays with women protagonists believed to have been written by women suffered the most discriminatory comments from women evaluators. They rated these plays and their characters least likely to be liked by audiences and to be produced.[240] Is it a perception that female written stories with female protagonists are too preachy or unrealistic, or is it that they more directly threaten the social order? The survey did not shed any light on this, but it did demonstrate that women artistic directors think that theater companies believe audiences will not respond as well to women writing about women.

Whether motivated primarily by competition or misplaced benevolence, women are not helping other women climb the ladder. Either way, it seems to be a chicken and egg situation that likely will not change until there is a perception among women that there are more career opportunities and fewer bottlenecks. Giving some women more power actually may make it more difficult for more women to gain power. As Former Secretary of State Madeline Albright famously said, "It would be better if more women were in office, but as far as peaceful goes: Just remember what high school was like."[241] (However, she also said, "There's a place in Hell reserved for women who don't help other women."[242])

The efforts of some women to hold back other women should be openly discussed, monitored and discouraged, just like racism, sexism, homophobia or any other attitude that holds a group back. This dirty little secret has to come out of the closet. One key to the solution may be the messages mothers are giving their young daughters.[243] In workplaces twenty years from now, will women who are in their twenties today treat the next generation of women the way they were treated? It's unclear, in part because feminism has not made changing this behavior a high enough priority. And that's the problem.

Paradox 6: Critical Mass Is a Myth.

So how many women does it take to change the status quo, given that they aren't always trying to advance the interests of other women? No, this is not one of those light bulb jokes. Many who write about gender issues speak of "critical mass" as the particular percentage of women in power in societal institutions that it will take for these women to be able to change those institutions and their policies toward a more feminist agenda. The term originated with nuclear fission, and describes the amount of concentrated radioactive material needed to start a nuclear chain reaction -- producing a great deal of energy from a relatively small amount of matter. But public policy is not subject to the precise laws of nuclear physics.

Feminism's political goals have been predicated in part on the notion that changes in laws affecting women and families would occur when critical mass was achieved. This is paradoxical because critical mass may not exist in any practical sense in this context. Since gender critical mass has not occurred in the real world, forecast percentages and timing are speculation – not based on actual experience and measurement of change. If feminism is waiting for change to come as a result of critical mass, we may have a very long wait.

An epidemic in a group of large primates had amazing consequences that cast critical mass prediction in a new light. Male savanna baboons establish dominance and rank using violent aggression. Primatologists began studying a troop of sixty baboons that lived near a garbage dump in 1979. Another nearby troop competed for access to the dump, but only the most aggressive males from that troop ate there. In 1983, tuberculosis-infected meat killed the entire troop closest to the dump and all the aggressive males in the other troop. With its aggressive males gone, the social dynamic of the surviving troop changed. Male savanna baboons normally bully females and lower ranking males, but after the deaths the remaining males restricted their violence mostly to males close to themselves in rank. Males also greatly increased the time they spent engaged in social grooming, an activity usually only favored by females. Troop members became much more congenial.[244]

The truly astounding thing is that when scientists returned a decade later none of the original surviving males remained, but the unique "pacifist" culture lived on. Female baboons stay in the troop and males migrate (the reverse migration pattern of great apes that live in large social groups). All of the males currently in the troop had emigrated in after the epidemic and apparently adopted the more congenial style they found there. The two-to-one ratio of females-to-males initially caused by the deaths continued in the pacifist troop, but scientists dismissed its cultural influence because males in other baboon troops with two-to-one ratios had the high social aggression typical of the species. The researchers also ruled out the possibility that pacifist males outside the group somehow had self-selected to join and remain in this gentler troop. Four more years of detailed observations were compared with another troop unaffected by the earlier TB fatalities. The researchers determined that after the troop's primary harassers died, females became unconditionally friendly toward both existing and new males. The males simply adopted this amicable "attitude."[245]

The baboons have shown us a model to significantly alter patriarchal norms: clear out the existing dominant males and then gradually reintroduce foreign males in an environment where females have had the freedom to behave differently. This scenario is not that far removed from what happened for four decades after Germany was split in 1945. During the Cold War, many men left the communist East for opportunities in the West. Germany "became a living experiment in social engineering," said *The New York Times*.[246] To recruit women at all levels in the workplace, East Germany provided daycare and after school programs unavailable to West Germans. The result was that Eastern women were able to blend careers and family responsibilities and assert themselves in ways unheard of in the West.[247]

By the time the Berlin Wall came down, employment rates for women were ninety percent in the East, but only fifty-five percent in the West. Today, Eastern women "are more likely to reach top management levels than women in the West," with the most notable example in government being German Chancellor Angela Merkel – an Easterner.[248] According to *The Times*,

> Eastern women are more self-confident, better-educated and more mobile, recent studies show. They have children earlier and are more likely to work full time. More of them are happy with their looks and their sexuality, and fewer of them diet. If Western women earn 24 percent less than men, the pay gap in the East is a mere 6 percent (though overall levels of pay are lower).[249]

Of course, it's hard to imagine how to intentionally implement a scheme eliminating large numbers of alpha men in a democracy. The most frequently suggested alternative is to significantly increase the ratio of women to men in policymaking bodies such as legislatures and boards that are filled with alpha males. But without removing much of the male hierarchy, just changing the ratio does not guarantee patriarchal policies will change. Wild chimpanzee groups[250] and baboon troops normally remain highly patriarchal even where there are twice as many adult females as males.

Women having majority control of an institution does not necessarily change the patriarchal paradigm. For example, in 2008 Rwandan women captured fifty-five percent of the seats in the national legislature, but the Rwandan army continued to be the worst outside actor in the war that began raging in Congo in 1998. Rwandan forces were exploiting Congo's mineral resources whilst killing its people, in a war that has seen an unprecedented level of rape and mutilation of women.[251] Women in the Rwandan Parliament either were unable or unwilling to use their power to stop this murderous exploitation. By 2010, Rwanda's government had devolved into a repressive dictatorship.

Benefits that might accrue from large percentage gains in women in power may be outweighed by other factors if the gains are attained too quickly. Implementing a huge leap in representation percentage to a supposed critical mass threshold, without changing anything else, sometimes can damage the affected institution. In 2002, when women were only seven percent of the board directors of its publicly traded companies, Norway enacted a law mandating that by 2008 boards of directors have at least forty percent women. But there weren't enough women available with anything close to as much business experience as the men they replaced.[252]

The Norwegian's initiative helped create what they call the "golden skirts." An "elite group" of seventy women soon held more than four board seats each. But that still did not bridge the newly created experience deficit in the minds of investors. A widely used measure of corporate health is Tobin's Q – market capitalization divided by asset replacement cost. The Tobin's Q of Norway's companies subject to the quota declined significantly, with the companies bringing on the most women directors faring the worst. And the newly reconstituted boards did not increase the percentage of female CEOs, which in 2010 remained unchanged from 2002 at five percent.

Undeterred by Norway's results, Holland and Spain will require compliance with their board quota laws by 2015.[253] Some companies in Britain voluntarily committed to attain thirty percent female boards by then, even though the founder of the initiative admitted it could "fizzle out."[254] France will require its publicly traded companies to have forty percent female boards by 2017, and in 2011 the President of the European Parliament threatened legislative action if European companies did not commit to attain that percentage by 2020.[255] But why these particular percentages or time frames? Why would the results be different than Norway's?

The New Hampshire Senate became the first legislature in U.S. history to be majority female in 2009: thirteen out of twenty-four senators. (The Democratic majority included eleven women). But no one has noted momentous changes resulting from this milestone, and by 2011 it was over. A Republican landslide left only six women in office.

Most feminists probably would not assert that critical mass had been achieved if the female majority in a legislature consisted of anti-feminist conservatives. Predicting what percentage of women in a particular institution will constitute critical mass for change is an elusive target, highly situationally dependent and inexact at best. There are no absolutes, but even a majority may not be enough. Change seems to occur slowly and is rarely subject to particular representation thresholds.

As described elsewhere in this book, paradoxically it may be that the greatest agents of change for women's power and influence are men. When men decide that more rights and influence for women are desirable, change happens most profoundly and rapidly. Women influence this change and their presence in institutions is often critical, but not because they have amassed a specific percentage.

| *A critical mass caveat:* | When the group at issue is small, say around a dozen people or less, it seems likely that in some situations there is a difference between having only one woman member versus three or more. The average corporate board size is eleven directors. A Catalyst study showed that having one or two women on a board of directors did little to change the board's culture or the policies it adopted. The one or two women on a board typically reported feeling isolated, and wanting to avoid not fitting in or being labeled as focused on female issues. Three or more women on a board felt more empowered to provide different perspectives, raise tough issues and work to change board processes. In 2006, fifteen percent of Fortune 500 companies had three or more women on their boards of directors.[256] By 2009, the percentage was nineteen percent.[257] |
| | The 2007 McKinsey study of the largest European companies bore out this rule of three. As reported by The *New York Times*, firms "with at least three women on their executive committees significantly outperformed their sector in terms of average return on equity by about 10 percent; operating profit was nearly twice as high."[258] (This data came from all over Europe and included only a few firms subject to Norway's quota.) |

Paradox 7: Beauty Matters More than Ever.

Both feminists and their detractors predicted that feminism would reduce society's obsession with female physical beauty as other factors such as political and economic power exerted greater influence on women's social status. But paradoxically, for better or worse, that does not appear to have happened. Part of the reason for this contrary result is that, gender aside, there is a broad cultural expectation that attractive people are smarter and more competent than less attractive people.[259]

For many reasons, however, appearance is more important for women than it is for men. First, because women are culturally conditioned to use beauty to their benefit in society, they are less likely to abandon this advantage over men. Second, evidence suggests that men around the globe, more so than women, are predisposed to favor mates who appear youthful and healthy.[260] Demonstrating the evolutionary importance of beauty, a psychologist conducting a forty year study in the U.S. found that beautiful women have more children than less beautiful women. Because of this, the proportion of women in the population considered beautiful is increasing. He also confirmed earlier findings that such women have a higher percentage of daughters than less beautiful women. He presumes this higher ratio is genetically driven, because beauty appears to be passed down from parents to children and is a more valuable trait in mating for women than for men. This is making women more beautiful the world over, he concludes.[q]

Third, beauty is an advantage in the workplace. In 2011, an industry financed study found that wearing tasteful makeup – what researchers call adornment or "the extended phenotype" – increases a woman's likability, competence and trustworthiness as perceived by both genders.[261] Even the National Organization for Women, a feminist icon, opposed a proposed tax on cosmetic surgery in 2009, arguing that because older women need to look younger to get and keep jobs they are greater consumers of such surgery than men.[262] Finally, multi-billion dollar profits ensure that the beauty industry will strive to perpetuate popular belief in the value of beauty.

Today, beauty and feminism do not appear to be locked in a struggle for supremacy. But if they were, feminism would be no match for beauty.[r] In 1983, sociologists Murray Webster and James Driskell predicted that the value of attractiveness would increase as the importance of gender and race in social status declined.[263] Earlier forecasts that progress towards gender

---

q. Leake. What is not known is whether skewing of sex ratios in countries such as India, discussed in Paradox 11, may be counteracting this trend. If beautiful Indian women are marrying up into wealthier families, and if those families tend more to use gender-selective abortions, beautiful mothers there may be having fewer daughters than less beautiful mothers married into less well off families less able to use costly in utero tests enabling gender-selective abortions.

r. The obsession with beauty does have a downside. Many cultures value thinness in women, presumably because this connotes youthfulness. Ads, television shows, catalogs and magazines scream "thin," "slim," "skinny" and "slender" in connection with food, diet, exercise, clothing and celebrity. A study found that ads for beauty enhancing products cause a lot of the women who view them to feel inadequate afterwards. Trampe. Many girls and women in the U.S. suffer from body image problems, and eating disorders are not uncommon. *Miss Representation* (Girls Club Entertainment 2011). *But see* Randall (asserting that many black women want to be fat).

equality would reduce women's attention to their appearance now seem naive.

Paradox 8: Sex Still Sells, and Sells Women Out.

If women are dressing and altering their appearance with cosmetics or surgery to please men, so the logic of feminism goes, it's subjugation. If the women are doing it to please themselves, it shows empowerment. The same logic is often expressed regarding sex. But the problem is, how do you know the difference?

The traditions of many cultures expect women to remain virgins until marriage and then to fulfill their husbands' sexual desires on demand. The more children produced, especially boys, the better. So, another goal of feminism was for women to gain control of their sexuality, for both gratification and reproduction. With the advance of the women's movement came more widely available birth control and abortion services. This decreased birth rates, delayed marriage and increased casual sex and divorce. *Sex and the City* soon followed.

But are women really in control? American society seems hypersexualized, but the focus – especially in youth culture – paradoxically remains on male gratification rather than women's. Even though sex is discussed more openly and seemingly is more available, the cultural context for women still is mostly about its use in "getting a man." The loudest headlines on magazines such as *Cosmopolitan* scream advice about heightening *his* pleasure. One of the hottest television shows in 2012, *Girls*, featured a lead character – played by the series' creator – in a relationship mainly focused on satisfying his various sexual fantasies, but that brought her little pleasure. And who would have predicted forty years ago that one of the biggest cultural trends in the twenty-first century would be the glorification of prostitution, and that college students would flock to *Pimp 'n Ho* parties with themes such as "pimps up, hos down"? Or that some very popular music would celebrate sexual violence against women?[s] Or that in 2008 a quarter of all office workers using computers connected to the Internet would spend some of their work day watching pornography,[264] thus further encouraging young women's image as male gratification machines.

The satiric film *Idiocracy,* based on consumerist cultural trends, portrays a distant future in which women's primary identity is defined by immediate satisfaction of men's sexual urges. It's an embarrassingly believable projection of current social mores. Such values are reflected in entertainment ventures such as the Lingerie Football League, founded in 2009 with professional teams in ten U.S. cities. Lean young women dressed only in helmets, shoulder pads, shoes and bikinis play full contact football in stadiums filled with cheering men.

But surely when one takes away consumer culture and business exploitation, objectification of women diminishes. A laboratory for this may be the annual Burning Man Festival on a Nevada

---

s. "Hos come, hos go, hos runnin ya slow, So keep her foot up in her ass, unless a dick in her throat, Main grew bitch will go what I make ya do." Snoop Dogg Presents Tha Eastsidaz, *Break A Bitch Til I Die, on* Duces 'N Trayz: The Old Fashioned Way (Doggy Style Records 2001)."Bitch hit that track, catch a date, and come and pay the kid. Look baby this is simple, you can't see. You fucking with me, you fucking with a P-I-M-P." 50 Cent, *P.I.M.P.,* Get Rich or Die Tryin (Shady/Aftermath/Interscope 2003). Further examples are presented in the documentary film Hip-Hop: Beyond Beats & Rhymes. The performance of *P.I.M.P.* by 50 Cent and Snoop Dogg during the 2003 MTV Music Video Awards featured women on leashes who were walked like dogs. An energy drink marketed by rapper Nelly is called "Pimp Juice." Thompson, C.

playa, or dry lake bed. Fifty thousand fans of counterculture congregate in a corporate-free community utilizing a gift based economy where the only commerce is altruism. Women participate in all sorts of ways, but in the evenings many wear a sort of rave party uniform: furry hat and below the knee leg warmers, bare thighs, panties and a short jacket over bare or barely covered breasts. In this utopian fantasy camp, such women are nicknamed "playa bunnies."

To repeat Nicholas Kristof's assertion, perpetuation and celebration of men's sexual values very much rely on women's adoption of such values.[265] Ariel Levy's book, *Female Chauvinist Pigs*, describes our "raunch" culture in which women gain status and power by wearing extremely revealing clothing, sexually performing in public or even by whoring. It's about being seen by and pleasing men on men's terms.[266] *Newsweek Magazine* ran a cover story in 2007 about how "bad girls" such as Paris Hilton, Brittany Spears and Lindsay Lohan affect the aspirations and behavior of pre-teens.[267] More and more girls think it's cool for their friends and admirers to see videos of them having sex with men they barely know. (*Newsweek* called them "prosti-tots.") But almost none of this, Levy complains, is about girls and women being in touch with their emotions or experiencing physical pleasure.[268] It's about girls seeking approval from boys. And this kind of approval has consequences. The teen pregnancy rate in the U.S. is the highest in the industrialized world.

It's a myth that our "liberated" sexual culture arose from the women's movement, as some conservatives have suggested in their ongoing historical revisionism. Rather the women's movement was in part a response to the interpretation of the sexual revolution already in progress by influences such as Playboy® king Hugh Hefner. In fact, some observers assert that feminism's inability to resolve an internal conflict over sex, especially pornography, killed much of the feminist movement's momentum in the 1980's. One group of feminists believed sex could not be separated from male domination. Another, "sex-positive" feminists, regarded sex on women's terms as liberating for women, but failed to gain mainstream acceptance.[t]

Feminism has failed to create a future in which women are sexual equals with men. This shortcoming may be wasting a lot female erotic energy. The research of Psychology Professor Meredith Chivers and others has found that women "have the capacity to be even more sexual than men," in part because women become sexually aroused by a wider range of stimuli.[269]

The myth that women are naturally monogamous	Do women instinctually try to enter into and maintain pair bonds? Regardless of whether that is true, it begs another question: does women's infidelity have an evolutionary basis? A primatologist observed that fidelity in primates "seems to occur only when males can impose it on females, either directly through their greater social power or brute force, or indirectly through controlling the resources that females and their offspring require."[270] No non-human primates that live in social communities practice monogamy.[271]

t. A literary example was provided by the memoir of a woman who placed an ad in the *New York Review of Books* that read: "Before I turn 67, next March, I would like to have a lot of sex with a man I like. If you want to talk first, Trollope works for me." Juska.

Anthropological evidence strongly suggests that women are not instinctively exclusively monogamous.[272] In hunter-gatherer societies, women are no less adulterous than men.[273] A score of primitive cultures even encourage women to be polyamorous to ensure that their children have multiple possible fathers, who by custom will provide for those children.[274] Women's fidelity in agrarian or industrialized cultures is the result of religious and cultural mores.[275]

Research showing that women are not exclusively monogamous naturally and seek genetic diversity (multiple partners) in mating includes:

- Genetic disease testing reveals that ten percent of children were conceived by men other than their presumed fathers.[276]
- A study of female college students shows that during ovulation they have more sexual fantasies about men who are not their partners.[277] Research also shows that women's faces become more attractive to others during ovulation,[278] and ovulating women tend to dress more provocatively.[279] (Men respond by being more attentive when their partners are ovulating,[280] possibly unconsciously tipped off by changes in the women's body odor.[281] One study also found a cold shower effect: men in committed relationships are less attracted to other women when they are ovulating.[282])

- Women are attracted to men with more masculine faces during ovulation, according to one analysis, but prefer men with softer features at other times.[283] Another study showed that women seeking affairs or short-term liaisons prefer men with more masculine faces, while for marriage, personality characteristics such as dependability and tenderness assume greater importance.[284]
- During ovulation, partnered female college students have a decided attraction to the body odor of other men with dominant personalities. The study found no preference in partnered women who were not ovulating, or in single women.[285]

Paradox 9: Women Who Serve Their Country Risk Rape.

Feminism sought to create a world where women had the opportunity to do any job open to men. Facing a "manpower" shortage after 9/11, the military actively recruited women to fill many positions formerly held only by men. But it did not protect many of those women from hazards that it knew or should have known about: their fellow comrades in arms. Servicewomen now have access to many jobs they can perform well regardless of their gender, but paradoxically cannot safely perform because of their gender. "A woman in the military is more likely to be raped by a fellow soldier than killed by enemy fire in Iraq," said Member of Congress Jane Harman in 2009.[286] It's outrageous that the greatest sacrifices made by some who served their country were exacted by soldiers in their own units rather than by the enemy.

Women have grown to constitute fifteen percent of those serving in the U.S. military, but they still face the double whammy of sexual violence and job discrimination. If a civilian employer knows that some employees who are members of a legally protected group face harassment or violence in the workplace because of their status, and the employer does not remedy the situation, that employer is liable for the injuries they suffer. But unlike civilian employers, the U.S. military is not subject to civilian discrimination laws. Military culture promotes combat aggression in part by promoting and exploiting male sexual aggression.[287] This helps explain why in 2002, believing that gender integration of the military was complete and concerned that a military committee advising the Pentagon on sexual assault crimes was fostering "radical feminism," the Pentagon replaced the committee's members and ended that part of its role.[288]

For decades military culture has tolerated and sometimes condoned sexual assault.[289] In 1991, 80 women were assaulted by drunken U.S. Navy pilots in what became known as the *Tailhook* scandal. One study of female U.S. veterans published in 2005 found that during their service in Vietnam or subsequent eras twenty-eight percent had been raped, with five percent having been raped on more than one occasion and five percent having been gang raped.[290] Those servicewomen assaulted or placed in fear that they would be often suffer from a form of post traumatic stress disorder now called "military sexual trauma."[291]

The military's failure to severely punish sex crimes sends a message to men. In 2003, a *Denver Post* investigation found that in the previous ten years, men in the Army charged with sex crimes such as rape or child molestation faced administrative proceedings nearly two and a half times more often than courts-martial.[292] In the Air Force Pacific command between 2001 and 2003, almost three times as many men charged with rape were processed administratively as tried by court-martial.[293] Why is this important? An administrative proceeding carries no risk of a criminal conviction or prison and allows a perpetrator to *re-enter civilian life with a clean slate.*[294] In 2004, U.S. Senators expressed outrage that in the Persian Gulf and elsewhere, the military seemed unable or unwilling to protect hundreds of servicewomen from sexual assault by their male colleagues, provide care to victims or punish perpetrators.[295] But by 2010, the military's message still had not changed. In that year, *Time Magazine* said eighty percent of military convictions for sexual assault result in an honorable discharge.[296]

The military finally established the Sexual Assault Response and Prevention program in 2005.[297] This may have been motivated by Congress directing the Defense Task Force on Sexual Assault in the Military Services to conduct a study of the problem in 2004, which it finally began in 2008.[298] *The New York Times* reported that fewer than forty percent of the alleged perpetrators of sexual abuse in 2008 were prosecuted, with forty percent of those facing court-martial and the rest administrative punishment.[299] But *Time* said in 2010 that only eight percent of the cases investigated are prosecuted.[300] The Pentagon estimates that as many as ninety percent of sexual assaults still are not even reported.[301]

A Government Accountability Office report in 2008 found that victims rarely reported assaults in part because they believed that they would be the only ones negatively affected by their doing so.[302] *The Report of Defense Task Force on Sexual Assault* admitted that a significant problem is that military Victim Advocates, unlike their civilian counterparts, are neither qualified nor certified to assist victims. Moreover, their conversations – that would be confidential under most states' laws – are not in the military.[303]

Women working for U.S. contractors in the Persian Gulf are at even greater risk. Why? Because the U.S. exempted military contractors and their hundred thousand employees from local law, and the U.S. is not enforcing U.S. law against them. The severest sanction facing private security guards that assault or rape is losing their jobs. Jamie Jones was gang raped in Iraq by Halliburton mercenaries in 2005, and imprisoned in a shipping container by her employer Halliburton after she reported the incident. She convinced a guard to let her call her father in Texas, who was able to prevail upon U.S. State Department officials to rescue her. The DNA evidence from her rape examination disappeared after U.S. Army doctors gave it to Halliburton. By the end of 2009, no law enforcement agency had conducted any investigation into the incident, and the perpetrators remained unpunished.[304]

If you thought this problem was caused mostly by the stress and chaos of combat zones, you would expect the risk to women to be less in the controlled academic environment of an officer training academy. But you would be wrong. In 2003, ten present and former female Air Force Academy cadets complained to a U.S. Senator that they had been sexually assaulted.[305] The Secretary of the Air Force subsequently estimated that at least ten percent of all women who attended the Academy in the past ten years had been sexually assaulted.[u] A former cadet who resigned after being raped "believed that *a majority* of women in the academy are raped or molested."[306] The uproar in Congress forced the

Pentagon to launch a special inquiry into the Academy's culture and values, where women felt "intimidated, inferior and overwhelmed."[307]

In 2003, one female cadet said a female

---

u. Schmitt with Moss. His statement may have been based in part on a 1997 survey of female cadets in which 10 percent said they had been sexually assaulted during the previous 12 months, with three-quarters of those victims of rape. Schemo with Moss. A survey of female cadets who graduated in 2003 found that 12 percent were victims of rape or attempted rape while at the Academy. Schemo, *Rate of Rape*.

Academy health counselor admitted to her group she had been raped twice, and warned them that although "it will probably happen to you," reporting it would end "your entire life at the Academy."[308] Not surprisingly, during the first twenty years the Academy admitted women, 1976-1995, no sexual assault victims filed an official complaint.[309] From 1996 until 2003, the 142 women[310] who reported being sexually assaulted often were told that their own conduct, such as drinking or socializing with superior officers, brought on the assaults. Many assault victims were charged with infractions for their conduct,[311] and many left the Academy after being hounded by peers and the administration.[312] Protecting male cadets' careers and the reputation of the Academy seemed to be the priority.[313] To make matters worse, the Air Force may have sent some victims a bill for the cost of the education they received before they left under duress.[314] Although fewer sexual assaults occurred at West Point – the U.S. academy for Army officers – victims there who did report described similar attacks on their conduct.[315]

Male domination also is deeply ingrained in U.S. military culture. Basic training teaches Marines to use misogynist slang: one's rifle is called "my bitch."[316] The Air Force Academy's large stone sign reading "Bring Me Men" wasn't removed until 2003.[317] The Academy's "entire belief system [is] that women are inferior," said a female cadet in that same year.[318] A Navy captain produced "chicks in the shower" videos, also containing gay slurs, which he repeatedly showed to all personnel onboard his aircraft carrier from 2006 to 2007. The Navy did nothing about it until 2011, when it relieved him of his command after a civilian newspaper put some of the videos on its website,[319] but he faced no reduction in rank or pay.[320] At military boot camps in the twenty-first century, male recruits who do not measure up still are derided by being called "girls" or "ladies,"[321] just as they were when I went to Army officer training school at Fort Bragg, North Carolina in 1973. Women face similar obstacles that gays do in the U.S. military: some see their presence as a threat to morale and combat effectiveness. This can become a self-fulfilling prophesy – the misogyny and fear of rape women face reduce their effectiveness.

Could a lawsuit break this bureaucratic blindness to safety and dignity? In 2011, fifteen female and two male victims of sexual assault in the military sued two Secretaries of Defense and the Department for flouting "Congressionally mandated institutional reforms."[322] One plaintiff was raped in Korea while serving with the Department's Criminal Investigative Command.

Sexual assault also infuses military culture to varying degrees in many other nations. The Israeli armed forces considered it a healthy part of military machismo for a male officer to have his pick of subordinate females as if they were his personal harem. This notion started to change after enactment of a law banning sexual harassment in 1998. High profile prosecutions followed, including rape charges brought against the Israeli President in 2006 followed by a seven year prison sentence imposed in 2011.[323]

The stories of the women who have been sexually assaulted are horrific, but the true cost of these harassments and assaults far exceeds their effect on women in the military. The military's incubation of violence against women also helps perpetuate this behavior in the far larger universe of civilian society. Having a macho military remains more important than ridding society of misogyny, a values choice feminism has been unable to change.

Paradox 10: The U.S. Holds Back Women's Progress.

It's ironic that the U.S., the country that is considered the birthplace of the modern women's movement, poses one of the greatest obstacles to international efforts to end gender inequality. Military and business interests enjoy a higher priority than the rights of women in most of the world, and this is especially reflected in U.S. foreign policy. While human rights movements confront moral and political issues, paradoxically women's rights and treatment often are left unquestioned as "cultural choices."[324] We react with outrage and disgust when in the U.S. a middle-aged married couple abducts an eleven year old girl off the street and the husband then secretly fathers two children with her. But when a similar thing happens in Afghanistan a hundred times a day, except that it's part of a bride price transaction, we collectively shrug our shoulders and say it's just a cultural thing.

A Truce for Women's Rights

The United States' poor track record in supporting international human rights is one reason it is less likely to lead global improvement in women's rights. America has consistently supported repressive governments, violated international human rights laws by executing criminals, opposed creation and operation of the permanent International Criminal Court that would prosecute human rights abuses, and has imprisoned and tortured hundreds of alleged terrorists for years without charging them with crimes or providing them access to lawyers.[325] Until overturned by the Supreme Court in 2005,[326] the U.S. was the only nation in the world with laws that allowed the execution of juvenile offenders.[327] According to Charles Grant, director of the Center for European Reform, "the European concern [is] that America doesn't believe in international law, doesn't believe in submitting itself to rules, organizations or norms that limit its freedom of action."[328]

An international treaty banning gender discrimination, the *United Nations Convention on the Elimination of All Forms of Discrimination against Women*, is intended to help "third world women gain their barest human rights."[329] It has been ratified by 185 countries, but has been unable to garner the two-thirds vote needed for ratification by the U.S. Senate since being signed by President Carter in 1980.[330] Part of the Senate's reluctance is that signatory nations agree to have their progress on women's rights assessed by an international panel every four years.

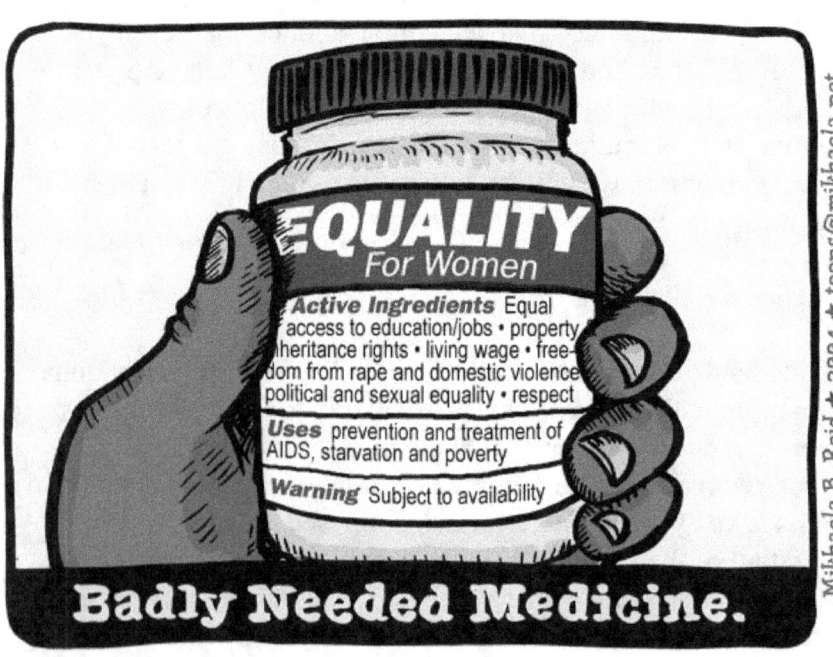

Mikhaela B. Reid ★ 2004 ★ toons@mikhaela.net

New York Times columnist Nicholas Kristof called America's alignment with fundamentalist Islamic nations in fighting expanded rights for women "an Axis of Medieval."[331] At regional U.N. conferences in Asia, Europe and the Americas in 2003 and 2004, the U.S. made unsuccessful attempts to substantially weaken international reaffirmations of the 1994 Cairo Consensus on providing sexual and reproductive information to women, known as the *Programme of Action of the United Nations International Conference on Population and Development*. At the Americas conference, the U.S. was alone in seeking changes that included the removal of all references to "reproductive health," "family planning services," "sexual health" and "condoms."[332] That same month, at a meeting of the U.N. Commission on the Status of Women, the U.S. was the only nation that refused to reaffirm the *Platform of Action of the 1995 World Conference on Women at Beijing*, which asserted the civil, educational and reproductive rights of women.[333]

From 2002 to 2004, the U.S. withheld all its financial support of the United Nations Population Fund, annually denying thirty-four million dollars of family planning services to women in the poorest regions of the world.[334] In 2005, at a U.N. meeting assessing international progress on the Beijing platform on its tenth anniversary, the U.S. attempted to pass a declaration that abortion is *not* an international human right.[335]

The *United Nations Convention on the Rights of the Child* declares that children have the right to survival, to development into fully functional adults, to protection from abuse and exploitation, and to full participation in cultural and social institutions. The *Convention* sets standards in health care, education, and legal, civil and social services. It is the most globally accepted human rights treaty in history – unratified by only two countries: Somalia, which did not have a functioning government for many years, and the United States.[336] (You may draw any appropriate analogies.)

A small step came in 2009 with the creation of the first Senate Foreign Relations Subcommittee on International Operations and Organizations, Human Rights, Democracy, and Global Women's Issues, chaired by Senator Barbara Boxer. Another step was Secretary of State Hillary Clinton's announcement in 2010 that the U.S. would for the first time allow its human rights record to be periodically reviewed by the U.N. Human Rights Council.[337] However, even if all of the Democrats and all of the Republican women in the Senate were to have voted for ratification of the globally accepted treaties to protect women, in 2010 – an optimum year for such a tally – that still would have been three votes short of the necessary margin. Unless U.S. voters see fit to elect at least sixty-seven senators that support international efforts to protect women – a radical change from the status quo – international leadership in women's rights probably will have to come from Europe or elsewhere. "America has been put to shame," said Tina Brown, editor of *Newsweek* and *The Daily Beast*. In 2012, "American women now have to look overseas for inspiration."[338]

What We Do Means More than What We Say

But who really cares about a bunch of treaties we've failed to sign, or international agreements we've tried to weaken? Isn't what we do more important?

Perhaps that's true, because sometimes what we actually do is worse than what we say. While we created legislatures in Iraq and Afghanistan with quotas requiring that twenty-five percent of the members be women – greater percentages than in the U.S. Congress – women's circumstances in these countries have declined since the U.S. invasions. Under Saddam Hussein's regime, Iraqi women "could drive, travel abroad alone, study in universities, serve in the army and work side-by-side with men.... They [chose] whom to marry and whether to marry at all."[339] Laws prohibited favoring men over women in inheritance and child custody disputes.[340] The war changed all of this. Islamic fundamentalists filled the power vacuum, seeking to use their strength on the U.S. created Iraqi Governing Council to replace secular law with religious law. Women suddenly had less freedom and fewer rights than before.[341] Parliamentary elections further increased the fundamentalists' legitimacy and power. Women's influence in the new "democratic" government steadily declined: in 2005 there were six women ministers and by 2011 only one – in charge of the ceremonial ministry of women's affairs.[342]

The consequences of U.S. involvement in Iraq followed the same pattern that occurred in Afghanistan in the 1980s, when the U.S. backed fundamentalist mujahideen, from which the Taliban later emerged, drove the Soviet Union out: women's status, freedom and rights plummeted. *Ms. Magazine's* Spring 2007 issue featured an article entitled, "The Talibanization of Iraq," that described how women have been largely driven underground in Iraq because they cannot safely leave their homes. With the absence of law and order and the rise of fundamentalist militias, women have been kidnaped off the streets, raped and killed in ever increasing numbers. Women who survive abductions have faced "honor killings" by their family members as a consequence of their possible defilement. Local fundamentalist decrees also subjected women showing any skin or hair in public to beatings by religious zealots.[343] The U.S. military "Surge" in 2007 improved women's safety in some areas of Iraq, but only came after women's rights and safety had been largely ignored for four years.

Three and half years after the U.S. invasion of Afghanistan, Amnesty International reported widespread domestic violence, forced marriage of women and girls under threat of death or imprisonment, and rape at the hands of local militias. The vast majority of school age girls were not attending school.[344] At the time the U.S. drove the Taliban from power in 2001, Afghanistan had the world's fourth highest rates "of both infant mortality and maternal death because of difficulties during pregnancy or during childbirth."[345] American occupation of Afghanistan has not improved the deplorable circumstances of women, including the seemingly intractable problem of religious proscriptions against women being treated by male doctors or training to become doctors themselves. In 2009, the rate of maternal mortality during childbirth in Afghanistan was the second highest on the planet and one in eight women there were dying during childbirth.

In 2006, President Karzai sent a proposal to the Afghan parliament to revive the Department for the Promotion of Virtue and the Prevention of Vice. This was the Taliban ministry whose enforcers barred women from employment or education, and beat women on the street who were not completely covered in conformance with religious law.[346] Shortly after Karzai made his proposal, the Taliban disemboweled and dismembered a teacher who refused to obey their orders to stop educating girls.[347] The Afghanistan Parliament in 2009 codified a version of religious family law to apply just to the Shia Islamist sect, despite the protests of human rights activists that it violated the constitution's guarantee of equal rights for women. Under the law Karzai signed, women must have their husbands' permission to leave the house, vote, seek work, go to school or visit the doctor, and they must provide sex to their husbands.[348]

There are two points to note in all this backsliding. The first is that religious fundamentalism will exploit social and governmental instability to push women backwards in time. The second and more important reality is that Western governments, especially the U.S., continue to tolerate this repression and seem to regard it as an acceptable outcome of their intrusion into non-Western societies.

Paradox 11: Abortion and Infanticide of Females May Be Increasing.

At the dawn of so-called second-wave feminism, which promised equal rights for women in the late 1960's, China had not yet implemented its one child policy. Almost no one in the west understood the extent of female infanticide in much of Asia, and tests to learn the gender of a fetus were not widely available in the developing world. So, no one could have predicted that the undesirability of female offspring would remain stubbornly pervasive in the twenty-first century, or that abortion and infanticide of females would be spreading. It's probably safe to say that only a dystopian science fiction writer such as feminist Margaret Atwood could have imagined it, and she would have been called a darkly pessimistic alarmist if she had. But it's not science fiction. It's very real.

The Dangers of Being Female in the Developing World

The oppression of women in the other parts of the world appears in American news stories occasionally, such as when the U.S. used the cruelty of the Taliban toward women to justify invading Afghanistan. The front page story about the female U.S. Air Force fighter pilot who sued the U.S. government for requiring her to "wear a black head-to-foot robe and ride in the back seat of any vehicle" when off her base in Saudi Arabia brought home the oppression facing Saudi women.[349] A Nigerian woman was sentenced to death by stoning for having a child out of wedlock.[350] Tales of wives being burned to death in India because their in-laws were displeased by the size of the dowry, or the state of the marriage or its issue, were confirmed by hospital statistics showing that three times more young Indian women are killed in fires than young men, and that police often cover up these deaths.[351]

Perhaps because the shock value of these stories has worn thin, we take for granted the harshness of patriarchy in much of the developing world and the seemingly insurmountable barriers facing women.[352] Women's comparatively smaller physical strength and size devalues them in economies that depend on manual work, because men are better able to perform many kinds of arduous physical labor. One study in Bangladesh showed that by age fifteen, a son's labor repays his parents for their total investment in him, while a daughter marries and moves away before ever reaching her parent's breakeven point.[353]

The sad fact is that in many developing nations, economic traditions make it dangerous simply to *be* female.[v] From the days of the Roman Empire to modern times in Asia and South America, daughter infanticide, sometimes called femicide, has been common.[354] The dark secret that neither the feminist or anti-abortion movements in the U.S. want to focus on in their debate is how abortion is now being used as a form of genocide against women. In India, where custom requires a bride's family to pay a hefty dowry to the bridegroom's parents, the modern practice is to abort a fetus if prenatal testing reveals it to be female. More abortions may follow until a couple conceives a male.[355] Before gender-selective abortion was criminalized, Indian clinics

---

v. There are some exceptions. On the island of Cheju Do, South Korea, many women work as *haeyno* – highly paid abalone divers. There, parents more highly value daughters over sons. Hrdy, MOTHER NATURE at 343. Japanese farmers in the eighteenth and nineteenth centuries preferred to have a daughter before having sons, so that the daughter could help raise a suitable heir. To achieve this result, called *ichihime nitarô*, parents used infanticide. *Id.* at 345.

advertised that the cost of fetal testing was only one percent of the cost of a dowry. In spite of its recent criminalization, the gender-selective abortion ban is rarely enforced. Ten thousand scanners capable of determining the gender of a fetus are sold to clinics in India each year,[356] and a 2011 study found increasing use of abortion to select for boys over the past two decades – especially by families with higher incomes and education.[357]

In societies that do not practice gender-selective abortion or infanticide, there are 105 live boys born for every 100 live girls.[358] (Due to lower female mortality rates and longer life expectancy, the gender ratio in such societies becomes even by about age 36 and reverses after that.[w]) In 2004 in several states in India, there were more than 125 boys in the 0-6 age group for every 100 females.[359] That same year, the overall ratio of live births in India was estimated at 113 boys to 100 girls. In 2007, the Indian government's call for parents to give their new born girls to orphanages rather than kill them failed to save the nearly one million girls who did not survive because of gender-selective abortion or infanticide.[360] In 2008, a survey found that in upper class urban areas of the Punjab state where expecting parents can easily afford fetal testing, there were just 300 girls for every 1000 boys.[361]

China's one-child policy is believed to encourage parents to sometimes kill or abandon female infants. Officially, 111 live boys were born for every 100 girls in 1990.[362] By 2004, that ratio had increased to 120 boys for every 100 girls.[363] A study released in 2009 estimated that there are thirty-two million more boys in China under the age of twenty than girls, and that the ratio of

---

w. Jones, M. There are 115 males conceived for every 100 females, but male fetuses face greater rates of miscarriage and stillbirth. Newborn boys are 25% more likely to die than girls, and sudden infant death syndrome is a 50% greater risk for boys. As teenagers, boys are twice as likely to die as girls, mostly from violence and accidents. *Id.*

young and middle aged men to women will increase in the future.[364] However, long-standing cultural prejudices may be a more powerful influence than the present one-child policy. In some areas of China during the eighteenth and nineteen centuries, boys outnumbered girls by more than fifty percent.[365] The power of this tradition is reflected in birth statistics in 2005 for households in rural China where a second child is permitted if the first is a girl. The ratio for those "second children" is 143 boys born for every 100 girls, which shows that gender-selective abortion or infanticide is common.[366]

Several Asian countries are exporting the practice of aborting females. U.S. Census data from the year 2000 shows that in Chinese-, Korean- and Indian-American families the ratio of boys to girls in second children is 1.17 to 1 if their first child is female. The ratio shoots to 1.51 to 1 for third children if the first two are female. Gender selection services advertise in newspapers targeting these cultures.[367]

According to an estimate in 1990, there were more than *one hundred million missing women* in the world that should have been alive but instead were aborted or did not survive childhood because of their gender.[368] That number should be larger today due to higher population growth in countries where femicide is common. Feminism is not only failing to put sufficient pressure on cultures and governments even to slow the growth of this extreme form of gender discrimination – it's also failing to influence parents in these life or death decisions.[369]

But what if an environmental toxin were responsible for the skewed ratio of boys to girls, rather than culture? For example, one economist asserts that a significant factor in the number of missing women is the prevalence of hepatitis B in some developing countries, because infected women on average bear more sons than uninfected women.[370] However, she admits that gender-selective abortion and infanticide might very well cause the same skewed ratios even if hepatitis B incidence were reduced. Indeed, vaccination has become far more widespread in developing countries, but gender birth ratios have worsened due to the greater availability of fetal gender testing.[371]

According to the coauthor of a study sponsored by Harvard University, these missing women threaten global security. She says imbalances in the ratio of men to women are creating a shortage of wives that could result in "marauding groups of under-educated testosterone-high" young men engaging "in stealing, gangs, bootlegging and terrorism."[372] The study is called *Bare Branches*, a Chinese expression for young men who will never marry or reproduce. It also uses historical data on gender imbalances to predict the rise of authoritarian regimes that will be more inclined toward war.[373]

The only Asian nation where gender ratios are coming back into balance is South Korea. Improvements in the status of women have been reinforced by government promotion of the slogan: "One daughter raised well is worth 10 sons!" In 1990, the same year the law guaranteeing that sons received the family inheritance was abolished, more than 116 boys were born for every 100 girls. By 2006, the ratio was 107 boys to 100 girls.[374]

In much of the world, the futures and living conditions of women that do survive often are determined by transactions in which women's economic value is set by men. In Pakistan, four men convicted of murder avoided the death penalty in 2002 by paying cash restitution and giving away eight of their daughters as brides to the victims' families.[375] That same year, two doctors in their forties married against the wishes of the bride's brother, who demanded women and cash from the bridegroom's family as compensation for the loss of her income. They refused to pay, and the couple had to "disappear" to avoid a death sentence ordered by a tribal council.[376]

Women without reproductive potential may have no value at all. Take the tragic tale of the first reported female Arab suicide bomber. Wafa Idriss divorced after she suffered a miscarriage and doctors told her she was infertile.[377] "It was a blow by the standards of Palestinian society, in which divorce is rare, divorced women are stigmatized and large families are prized. Of the 35 girls in her grade school class, she was the only one to be divorced and one of just two without children."[378] It was no wonder she wanted to die, and why men encouraged her – she was worth little, except as a martyr. Three Chechen women who blew themselves up in the Moscow subway and in two airplanes in August 2004 faced this same social worthlessness. Living in a Muslin culture that stigmatizes childless wives, they were divorced because they were unable to conceive.[379] Female suicide bombers are known as "black widows" in Russia, because some were married to Chechen guerrilla fighters killed by security forces.[380]

In many areas of the world, girls and young women who survive selective birthing practices and are not forced into pseudo-slavery in oppressive marriages still risk being sold  as sexual slaves.[381] Many will die of AIDS.[382] Columnist Nicholas Kristof estimated in 2011 that more than ten times "as many girls are now trafficked into brothels annually as African slaves were transported to the New World in the peak years of the trans-

Atlantic slave trade."[383] In 2004, UNICEF reported that the sixty-five million girls kept out of school worldwide face increased risks of extreme poverty, and of death in childbirth or from AIDS.[384] Without greater economic and political power, most women in the developing world are doomed to remain enslaved as the weaker gender. If they learn about feminism at all, it likely will be presented to them as an evil force bent on destroying their culture and traditions.

PART TWO: The Solutions

"The main thing about feminism is that it is a constant puzzle. You have to keep thinking it through."
Debbie Stoller[385]

By insisting that women and men are identical, not taking into account that egalitarianism favors men's competitiveness, and failing to address the decline in women's happiness and their lack of control over their sexuality, feminism has lost its way. By assuming that women would always be more interested in bringing down patriarchy rather than each other, relying on the notion that merely increasing women's presence in institutions will form a critical mass that will reform those institutions, and not pressing hard enough to elevate women's rights to basic human rights rather than a mere cultural value, feminism has not planned to succeed. It has not articulated a coherent strategy to attain gender equality and overcome the stronger forces of prejudice and misogyny.

These last four chapters suggest ways to resolve some of the eleven paradoxes. Some restate old ideas, while others are new approaches to breaking patriarchal inertia. The first of these final chapters suggests mechanisms to change the world one woman at a time through increasing economic opportunities, balancing work/life demands, and mentoring. The next chapter asks the question: aren't women's rights also human rights? Shouldn't we promote women's rights abroad, and especially target reducing rape? At home, pro-women media campaigns could help young women transform their expectations and self image, and change hearts and minds about women's roles.

Nations that emphasize social safety nets and human rights in the broad sense – rights to food, shelter, education, employment, health care and peace – have the highest percentages of women in elective office. Many of these priorities particularly help women, even though they have nothing overtly to do with women's rights. Chapter fourteen describes why the U.S. may not be able to increase women's participation in leadership in government much above current levels until we adopt public policy priorities aligned with the public's perception about women's public policy priorities and leadership skills. And when we allow gay marriage, this will demonstrate that we are ready to leave behind some of the gender role stereotypes that have held women back. Will we do these things? It's not at all clear. But increasing justice, fairness, and public safety would be reason enough, even if the general public were not motivated to make broad changes solely to advance the cause of women.

If we achieve these conditions necessary for women's advancement and women's participation in government continues to rise only very slowly, chapter fifteen describes a quota system intended to accelerate the pace. As most of the world's democracies have demonstrated, legislative gender quotas and recruitment of more activists can accelerate change and take things to a new level. But there are significant risks in using quotas before conditions are ripe for their effectiveness.

The chicken and egg problem affects a few of these suggestions. Women cannot advance as rapidly without these changes, but neither will some suggestions likely be adopted as long as men remain substantially in charge of political and economic institutions. But we have to start somewhere.

Chapter 12. Resolving the Paradoxes by Helping Individuals

"If your society is upside down, you turn it upright! If a little girl has a problem you help her. I don't think it's heroic. I think it's just living." Nobel Lauriate Leymah Gbowee

The most direct way to promote women's influence may be helping individual women reach their full potential. And, whether or not you believe it desirable to have more women in positions of power and influence, changes that empower individuals also would benefit our society in other ways.

Universal Mentors and Training for Women and Girls

Nearly two generations have passed since the activism began that launched the modern women's movement and changed our laws and national conscience. But still:

- The U.S. teen pregnancy rate is the highest in the industrialized world.[386]
- Prostitution is attracting more girls than ever before, compounded by sex trafficking.
- The difference in median income between women and men working full time remains higher than twenty percent,[387] and is getting worse for those in some professions.
- The number of women penetrating management and

leadership positions is small and only growing at a snail's pace.
- Recent studies across scores of cultures have shown that men are benefiting more than women from prosperity and progressive institutional changes in the most advanced nations. Behavioral and personality differences between men and women are getting greater, not smaller, as cultures evolve, and these changes are helping men better take advantage of greater opportunities at the expense of women's advancement.
- Work/life balance conflicts show no signs of abating.

We need a national commitment to mentor every girl and young woman in America. The word "mentor" comes from the ancient tale *The Odyssey*. Mentor – actually the goddess Athena disguised as an old man – advised the son of Odysseus in his quest for leadership in his father's absence, helping him achieve success. But girls and women often are left out of the old boy networks that traditionally provide mentoring in our society. Providing a mentor to every girl and young woman would help fully realize the unique contributions women can make to our culture, our economy and our democracy. One-to-one mentoring works – all the data on better outcomes for youth proves it. If more women are to attain positions of influence and power, mentoring is key.

MentorHer[SM] is a suggested overlay program to help create and maintain a national recognition that the process of raising a girl to midlife womanhood should include a mentor.[388] This overlay would fill the gaps between existing programs by directly connecting more mentors and mentees with outreach and recruitment. It would provide training, certification and on-going enrichment to the efforts of its own and other programs' mentors. Mentors are more effective when they regularly share their experiences with other mentors and enhance their skills through continuing education programs.

For every girl to have a mentor, every young woman should be a mentor. To ensure supply meets demand, every woman in her thirties should mentor two women, every woman in her forties should mentor three women, and every women in her fifties should mentor four. Beyond that age, women should take on as many mentors as their time and skills allow.

The United States, even though founded by the elite intellectuals of the time, originally embraced egalitarian principles. Nearly two hundred years later, a wave of anti-intellectualism found new strength during the Nixon administration and additional amplification during the regimes of Ronald Reagan and George W. Bush.[389] Although a number of Ivy League universities pride themselves on their graduates' contributions to public policy, the idea of educating managerial civil servants in elite academies – as they do in Europe – has never gained traction here.

But why not create graduate level programs dedicated to training women to be the public policy and business leaders of tomorrow? A platform for this could be one of the best all women's schools in America, such as Barnard, Smith, Mt. Holyoke or Wellesley. How about a rich donor dropping $100 million to endow the Hillary Clinton School of Public Policy at her alma mater Wellesley College?[x] Or, if Oprah were so inclined, she could build and endow the Oprah School of Public Policy. But the window for action may not be open for long. After anti-

---

x. Admitted problems with Hillary Clinton's legacy are that some of her initial gravitas as a Presidential candidate and as Secretary of State relied on her husband's, and that she was vilified by some women on the right, but a movement has to chart and cherish its progress and she is an undeniable part of that progress.
On the subject of policy academies, how about a national graduate school for government management open to both genders? It could be kept non-partisan, just as the military academies and war colleges have been (with some exceptions at the Air Force Academy).

intellectualism has waned, historically it has been reasserted as a vehicle for political gain – and that pattern was illustrated in 2010 with a vengeance.[390]

Universal Ceiling-less Part Time Career Tracks

If our economy is to obtain the maximum benefit from the millions of women trained and educated to create, produce, process, diagnose, teach, manage or advise, can't we offer options that will allow them to continue to work if they choose to have families? For many American workers today, good jobs with work schedules that accommodate child or elder care responsibilities are scarce.[391] Even worse, they appear to be diminishing. The percentage of employers offering flextime or job sharing *dropped significantly* between 2001 and 2004, according to a survey by the Society for Human Resource Management.[392]

Where American employers do allow flexible work arrangements for child and elder care, employees often find that taking advantage of them negatively affects advancement.[393] Catalyst reports that women, "whether by choice or necessity, make that trade-off, whereas men do not."[394] A 2008 survey of employment laws in twenty-one countries, including Australia, Canada and the most developed nations of Europe, ranked the United States *dead last* in workplace flexibility for balancing family responsibilities.[395]

Creating workplaces that enable women to stay engaged in their professions without long interruptions is important because advancement into leadership positions depends on having years of experience. If women are forced to leave their jobs in order to have children, most will never recover those lost years in their careers in either salary or advancement. At the age when many men are reaching the pinnacles of their careers, many women are struggling to reenter the workforce with unequal experience.

Providing part time work options in every career track would reduce this disparity and ensure that the greatest number of women are poised for leadership roles when they are done having children.

When layoffs began in earnest in 2008 in response to the Great Recession, there was much public debate about the merits of simply reducing many workers' pay and hours to less than full time in order to reduce the need for layoffs. Proponents argued that shortening hours in this way would substantially decrease the number of families in dire economic circumstances, spread the pain of the recession more equitably, and lessen the chances the economy would spiral into a free fall. Opponents argued that layoffs are an essential mechanism by which employers eliminate underperforming workers.

In Germany, if companies reduce workers' hours involuntarily, the government uses money from a special fund to pay workers two-thirds of their lost salaries. This is called *Kurzarbeit*, which translates as *short work*.[396] Hopefully, by the time you are reading this, the economy will be moving out of recession, but if not, or in future economic downturns, perhaps this approach has merit in the U.S. If it could jumpstart a change in employers' attitudes toward letting employees work less than full time schedules, we'd not only be better able to weather downturns, we'd also have a more flexible and family friendly economy.

Does the idea of widespread part time work seem crazy and unworkable in boom times in the U.S.? Requiring government and business to offer and culturally normalize part time work may seem like a leap to remedy the lower wages and fewer promotions that women experience. But undoing discrimination will require ingenuity, especially because U.S. resolve to fully remedy gender discrimination lags far behind that of many nations with developed economies. Until their child is eight, Swedish parents can work an eighty percent schedule.[397] Since 2000 all Dutch

workers have had the right to a four-day week,[398] and in 2010
three quarters of female workers and a third of male workers were
part timers.[399] France reduced its workweek partly to shift away
from "cultural patterns in which women … take more
responsibility than men for providing care to children, other
relatives, spouses, and themselves."[400]

England takes a voluntary approach that requires an employer to
give serious consideration to an employee's request for "flexible
working" to care for a child or closely related adult. Businesses
can refuse to honor a request for flex time, job sharing,
telecommuting or reduced hours if it would, among other things,
impose additional costs or reduce production, quality or
performance.[401] A 2005 survey of all requests, not just those
covered by the law, found that in the preceding two years
fourteen percent of employees requested flexible working, with
women asking at a much higher rate than men. In spite of their
power to say no, employers accepted more than eighty percent of
requests. But the same survey found that less than two-thirds of
workers knew of their right to ask.[402] What is not known is how
many employees wanted to make requests but feared the career
consequences of doing so.

Providing longer maternity and paternity leaves has been
suggested as a means to equalize career opportunity and would be
appreciated by many parents, but that does not offer a real
solution to balancing family and work for most women. The
Scandinavian experience in offering long periods of such leave is
a cautionary tale for women's career advancement, and for why
part time employment must be normalized and available if
women are to penetrate the upper ranks of management in larger
numbers. The Swedish authors of a 2009 study found a
correlation between paid parental leaves exceeding one year and
slower career progress. It noted that women's representation in
management is higher in English speaking countries than in
Nordic nations and suggested the length of maternity leaves as a

reason.[403]

An important lesson of the 2008 economic collapse is that the short term focus of market forces sometimes must be redirected by longer term public policies initiated by government. Business and government employers don't seem to be recognizing the value of keeping women in the workforce. There aren't enough employers offering part time tracks for people seeking such work. If job seekers don't have meaningful choice, there is little or no pressure on employers from market forces. What if the U.S. allowed any employee of all but the smallest employers to work a part time schedule of at least thirty hours a week, at a proportionate wage to full time and with eligibility for health benefits? To be fair, access to such a schedule would have to be available to all it were available to any.

The forty hour work week is just a convention. The length of the work week varies from culture to culture, from profession to profession, and across time. It may be argued that it is too expensive for business and government to employ legions on schedules of thirty hours a week,[y] but the forty hours standard in America was arbitrarily pegged long ago in government fiats and union bargaining. Why couldn't the paradigm shift over several years as the average number of hours worked per week declined? The wages of those voluntarily working less than forty hours a week would be proportionate to the reduction in their hours, but more people would be employed.

Congress could enact remedies as it has done in the past to correct other discriminatory economic inefficiencies. Business and government agencies could be required to incorporate part time employees into the critical path of all their functions. For

---

y. Although businesses' overhead costs could increase if there were more employees, reduced turnover and retraining costs might balance that out.

those employees exempt from overtime rules, this means that as critical projects pass through an entity, career part time workers would be involved in them at all levels and obligated to work extra time as needed to meet agreed upon objectives – similar to the demands placed on full time exempt workers – but proportionate to their reduced schedules. Such a rule would preclude there being key channels in business, consulting or creative processes that only full time employees service. Why is this important? Without this requirement, part time workers would be marginalized as second class, now a frequent complaint of women who exercise a part time option – often called the "mommy track." Also, it would go a long way toward reducing the resentment full time workers sometimes feel toward part time workers because of big differences in how much work intrudes into their respective personal lives.

There are two steps to making part time work accessible to all. The first is removing the considerable disadvantages often faced by part time workers. The 1997 European Union Directive on part time work (97/81/EC) largely did that by guaranteeing part time employees treatment equal to full time employees, including pro rata equal compensation and benefits such as paid leave and retirement.[404] Law in European Union nations, New Zealand and Australia also recognizes that because most part-time workers are women who work part time only because of family caregiving obligations, disparate treatment of any part timer in the workplace is gender discrimination.[405]

Academia should provide extended tenure tracks, so that aspiring professors do not have to choose between having a family and meeting rigid up or out deadlines many universities impose on junior faculty.[406] Partner track professions such as law would need to provide similar extensions. Employers also could be required to provide on ramps – reinstatement to full time status with six months' notice from the employee. (In order to minimize disruption, employees could be limited to making a switch only once a year.)

The second step is providing actual access. One means to increase part time work would require that businesses and governments receiving federal money offer part time work options sufficiently appealing so that target percentages of workers choose them. There are few restrictions on the ability of Congress to place conditions on the use of federal dollars. A more ambitious plan would enact a tax on businesses that fail to offer attractive part time options.

Another idea is the Working Families' Flexibility Act, first introduced in Congress in 2007, co-sponsored by Senators Kennedy, Clinton and Obama and modeled after similar successful laws in the U.K. and other European nations. Still dormant after three sessions, the bill would require employers to consider all workers' requests for reduced or flexible hours.[z] (California and a few other states already require state agencies to offer "reduced worktime" to "the extent feasible," and guarantee part time workers pro rata pay and benefits.[407]) Many European nations go a step further for caregivers and provide them with the right to part time schedules in all jobs. However, Germany, France, Belgium, and the Netherlands set the gold standard by providing all employees the right to work part time, with unreasonable employer refusals subject to legal review.[408]

Through grassroots action, citizens can hasten the day when part time work is available as a career option without stigma. They can write and email legislators, vote for candidates supporting this policy, and donate their time to organizations working toward this goal. How about creating an organization dedicated solely to

---

z. http://maloney.house.gov/issue/working-families-flexibility-act. Despite the fact that the bill's author, Rep. Carolyn Maloney, represents part of Manhattan, as of 2012 *The N.Y. Times* had never written an article mentioning the bill.

that purpose? I've got a name, the National Part Time Work Association, and a website, www.nptwa.com.

For professional part time work to really gain acceptance in the U.S. may require that men demand and take advantage of it themselves.[409] Government may have to create incentives of the sort that Sweden did to boost the percentage of men taking paternity leave. If a couple uses the thirteen months of state paid parental leave, each parent must use at least two months. Because of this rule, eighty-five percent of fathers use some of the leave to be with their children. This has helped integrate parental leave into business culture and greatly reduced its detriment to career paths, as well as helped better integrate fathers into family life. In one survey the biggest resistance to paternity leave came not from fathers but from mothers, who saw it as encroaching on their baby time.[410] Iceland went further, requiring each parent to use at least three of the nine months of parental leave guaranteed to every family.[411]

Part time work is important for another reason affecting us all. *The Atlantic's* widely read July 2012 cover story, *Why Women Still Can't Have It All*, observed that workplace structures make it almost impossible for mothers to have high pressure, long hours careers. Author Anne-Marie Slaughter wryly noted that, "In Washington, 'leaving to spend time with your family' is a euphemism for being fired" for men, but is often the truth for women.[412] Writer Anand Giridharadas responded that America may actually be worse off for being governed and managed by "single-minded, obsessive, fierce, hurried … self-serving [and] less-than-empathetic" alpha career types who largely "ignore their families." He rightly wondered what biases affect policymakers who "have prioritized the making of social policy over their own families."[413]

Humanizing Part Time for Hourly Workers

Sixty percent of U.S. workers are hourly.[414] But if you're not an hourly worker in retail or manufacturing, you may not be aware of the increasing popularity with employers of what is called *just in time scheduling*, which encourages first line managers to wait until the last possible minute to post schedules that vary each week. It is especially common in businesses that use a high percentage of low skilled, part time workers. It was originally intended to give employers an advantage in industries with rapidly fluctuating labor needs and high employee turnover, and also to spread the pain of working less desirable evening and night shifts across a larger number of workers. As described in an insightful analysis by The Work Life Law Center at Hastings College of the Law, this scheduling is callous and misguided, further increases turnover and pushes up labor costs.[415] It greatly increases the stress on families trying to arrange child and elder care.[416] It sends a message to many employees that their work/life issues don't matter, and thus as employees that they don't really matter either.

The Center's report, available free on the Internet, provides tools for employers to address varying labor demands and at the same time reduce turnover by better accommodating employees' family issues. One of its most significant findings was a survey of retail stores that found that total hours worked varied in the average store by only three hours a week, meaning that business conditions often may not justify the use of just in time scheduling.[417] There is no need to put an entire workforce through the pain of last minute scheduling to accommodate such a small weekly change. Another finding is that many just in time workplaces employ many more than an optimal number of workers, and give those workers far fewer hours then they would prefer.[418]

The report's suggestions would benefit all hourly workplaces.

First, employers should survey their staff to determine individual shift and scheduling preferences, and then build a medium or long term schedule around those preferences. With schedule predictability, many employers will find they can give more hours to a smaller workforce and reduce turnover. To handle fluctuations in demand and employees' family emergencies, the report suggests allowing shift swapping, flexible start times, and using floaters to cover emergencies. Online scheduling is very inexpensive and lets employees easily find substitutes to cover for them. The best way to handle overtime needs is to ask for volunteers, and if that does not fill the need, then use a coupon system that has employees on call no more than one week a month.[419] That might seem preferable to employers than guaranteeing caregivers the right to refuse overtime, which is the law in Norway, France and Switzerland.[420]

Universal Affordable Daycare

Another key element in keeping mothers active in the workforce is quality, affordable daycare. Many parents say that they cannot find daycare that is both. That's partly because the U.S. does not subsidize child care for working mothers, unlike the governments of Canada and most European countries.[421] France goes even further: all French children ages three to six go to state sponsored daycare for some part of the day, even if their mothers are not working.[422] (Not all of Europe is progressive in this way. In Germany, only six percent of mothers with two or more children had returned to work full time in 2009. Trying to reverse its having the highest percentage of childless women in Europe, Germany is rapidly introducing daycare.[423])

Quality preschool childcare benefits both parents and kids. A forty-year study concluded that U.S. Head Start preschool programs have enormous benefits that are especially noticeable when the children in those programs reach age forty, as compared to similarly situated children who have not been in Head Start.

From educational achievement and income to crime avoidance and family stability, every measure was better. An investment of $15,166 per child in preschool paid back society over $250,000 (adjusted to the value of the dollar in the year 2000), a return of more than seventeen to one.[424] Yet, only a few U.S. states offer universal preschool for all four year olds.

Government could subsidize good daycare on a sliding scale so that parents of limited means can afford it. Subsidies would enable more adults to work and thus contribute to the economy rather than being a drain on it. Subsidies for senior daycare also would help many who take care of their parents become more fully employed. During times when government is trying to stimulate the economy, funds for daycare quickly would create jobs for daycare workers.

Economic Development Abroad

Where women are able to earn income outside the home, their status and power in the family increases and this in turn influences culturally driven attitudes about women's rights and freedoms.[425] Part of the reason for this is that women who are less socially and economically dependent are better able to leave men who engage in risky or abusive behaviors. The more women are empowered economically, the greater social and political influence they have.

The international community could do more to improve the lives of women in the developing world. Progress will require funding for educational programs, development of manufacturing and service economies, and loans and advice for women starting small businesses.[426] (This may be true in America as well. Twice as many women as men start their own businesses and many more would succeed with financial assistance.[427])

2006 Nobel Peace Prize winner Muhammad Yunus' model of

lending small sums to enterprising Bangladeshi women has been wildly successful. "Telephone ladies" buy cell phones and earn money in poor villages by taking messages and making calls for others. Women buy a cow or some chickens and sell milk or eggs. Instead of begging, beggars buy a basket of goods to sell. Farmers buy more land to attain a profitable economy of scale. Aspiring merchants buy a stall from which to sell their wares. The business ventures such loans make possible improve the lives of women and their children.[428] Micro lending should be further expanded to include more women all over the globe.

The biggest barrier to educating girls in the developing world is school fees, which poor families (half the world's population[429]) either cannot pay or choose not to pay in lieu of educating their sons. In societies in which a married woman goes to live with her husband's family, some parents say that paying to educate a daughter is "like watering a neighbor's garden."[430]

The World Bank used to encourage poor nations to collect fees to pay for textbooks, but abandoned the policy in 2002. Often, the costs of collecting school fees are as great as the revenue they bring, so the fees do not provide significant net income for schools. Several African nations abolished fees and their school enrollments soared.[431] In Pakistan, where in 2003 the percentage of girls attending high school was only twenty percent and less than one-third of women could read, officials in Punjab province abolished school fees and began to pay girls who stayed in school after the fifth grade a stipend of about four dollars per month.[432] Developed nations should pledge to increase their international aid to fill any income gaps developing nations face from abolishing these fees.[433] Better yet, they should assist developing nations in offering school stipends to girls.

Stipends may have another benefit. A study in Malawi gave young women aged thirteen to twenty-two and their families small monthly stipends of from five to fifteen dollars.[434] This resulted in their delaying having sex, reduced their frequency of sex and number of partners, and cut the rate of their contracting AIDS or herpes in half. Girls that did not get such payments were much more likely to exchange sex for "gifts" or money.[435]

Undoubtedly, there are other ways to increase girls' school success, but empirical research should support the expenditure of substantial aid dollars. *New York Times* columnist Nicholas Kristof says that another essential step in getting more girls educated at rural schools is to provide menstruation assistance – toilets and free sanitary napkins. Without these simple things, he asserts, menstruating girls often miss school, fall behind and drop out.[436] A controlled study in Nepal did not support his claim,[437] but more study is needed.

When Algeria won its independence from France in 1962, the new government encouraged families to send their girls to school. Forty-five years later women comprise only twenty percent of the workforce, but seventy percent of the lawyers, sixty percent of judges, and a majority of the doctors.[438]

If we decide that it is important for women to be fully integrated into all levels of society, we're going to have to actually plan to attain that goal. It seems unlikely to happen organically. Mentoring women, accommodating motherhood by offering sane, less than full time work schedules, providing affordable and available childcare, and assisting women entrepreneurs around the globe are all necessary and sensible paths toward gender equality – and fairness.

Chapter 13. Resolving the Paradoxes with Women's Rights

"I firmly believe that the central moral challenge of this century, equivalent to the struggles against slavery in the 19th century or against totalitarianism in the 20th, will be to address sex inequality in the third world." Nicholas Kristof[439]

Providing the assistance described in the previous chapter won't necessarily change hearts and minds. That will require several separate efforts. Advertising and public relations campaigns are important mind changers for any issue, and are especially important to counter other destructive messages in media and popular culture. Taking strong moral stands on key gender issues also is critical. Rape should not be tolerated anywhere in the world, and women's rights should be universal – not mere cultural artifacts that change from border to border.

Media Campaigns

In 2008, Al Gore announced a three hundred million dollar advertising campaign intended to motivate consumers to become activists in the fight to slow climate change.[440] Supporters of increasing women's power and influence should plan a similar campaign to achieve their goals, and include many forms of media entertainment beyond advertising.[441] Why? Many media images reinforce and perpetuate patriarchy. What are the most pervasive messages girls and women get from the web, magazines, television and films? That being pretty, thin, and attached to a man are women's most important aspirations in life. Part of the proof of this is that girls eight to twelve years old spend over half a billion dollars a year on beauty products in the U.S., and teens spend over a billion. One survey revealed that over eighty percent of ten year old girls are afraid of getting fat.[442]

But what's the most important message that's mostly absent? That women can competently be in charge of businesses or governments. The only Hollywood film ever to portray a female American President was the 1964 comedy, *Kisses for My President*, in which the President "happily resigns when she becomes pregnant."[443] In 2005 the ABC television network finally rolled out a drama series called *Commander-In-Chief*, about a woman Vice-President who assumes the office after the President dies. It lasted one season. Television science fiction has been more sympathetic, with *Battlestar Galactica* and *Star Trek Voyager* positively portraying powerful female leaders. But you have to contrast these with horror films such as *John Carpenter's Ghosts of Mars (2001)* in which matriarchy is a nightmare.[aa] Taken together, these messages and missing messages help maintain the discomfort many have about gender equality and female leadership.[444]

But wait, didn't the U.S. come very close to electing a woman as President in 2008? Perhaps, but an NBC poll after Hillary Clinton began her campaign early in 2006 found that twenty-seven percent of registered American voters were not likely to vote for a female candidate for President in 2008, with forty-one percent of

---

aa. One of the first science fiction matriarchies appeared in 1915 in Charlotte P. Gilman's book *Herland*. All the men in a mythical remote country had marched off to fight a war, and a volcanic eruption simultaneously killed them and cut off access to the rest of the world. A scientific breakthrough enabling virgin birth of females spawned a peaceful society in which women do just fine without men.

those listing "women are not up to the job" or "it's a man's job"
as their main reason.[445] Clinton's personal unpopularity with
conservatives could have been a factor in the results – so another
early 2006 poll by CBS attempted to tease out the Hillary factor.
Ninety-two percent of respondents (not necessarily voters) said
they would vote for a woman of their own party for President, but
only fifty-five percent thought other voters were ready for a
female President. This is a method pollsters often use to uncover
bias when survey respondents are reluctant to admit it. People
say, "Sure, I'm happy to support [candidate or cause], but other
voters are biased and will never go for it." This indicates that
their own inclination to vote for a woman may be weak. After
Clinton's run fizzled in May of 2008, *The New York Times* could
not find a political strategist able to name anyone else likely to
become the first woman President.[446]

One approach for elevating media portrayals of women relies on
power, while the other depends on money. Marie Wilson of *The
White House Project* says that actors with pull in Hollywood,
women who are big box office draws, should demand scripts
about women who have achieved positions of power in business
or politics and whose courageous and responsible use of that
power makes them excellent role models for teenagers. Big male
stars should announce they are eager to play supporting roles in
such films.[447] Wilson wants films made that will help build
popular support for her goal of having a woman in the White
House. The biggest stars may be able to have some influence in
this way.

Under the money approach, wealthy supporters of women's
equality could use their fortunes to finance long-term TV
advertising campaigns aimed at influencing young people to
support equality both politically and in their own lives. There is
hardly a person in the United States over the age of fifty that does
not remember the anti-littering and anti-pollution television ad
campaign of the 1970's featuring the crying Indian that helped

spawn Earth Day and the environmental movement. In 2008, Microsoft founder Bill Gates and New York Mayor Michael Bloomberg announced their five hundred million dollar initiative to get people to stop smoking.[448] Why not similar efforts to change attitudes about gender inequality? If no benefactors step forward, perhaps a special tax on punitive damages awarded in gender discrimination or sexual harassment law suits could publicly finance a campaign.

Looking for economic justifications for such campaigns? How about a decline in the long term social costs of teen pregnancy and reduction of the treatment and criminal justice expenses stemming from rape and domestic violence? The annual cost of teen pregnancy to U.S. taxpayers is estimated to be over nine billion dollars,[449] so a six percent reduction would save governments more than five hundred million dollars a year. Just a one percent reduction in domestic violence in the U.S. would save an estimated six hundred and seventy million dollars each year.[450] These potential savings are just some of the powerful justifications for hundred million dollar advertising campaigns.

Advertising works – how anti-smoking ads are a greater influence on behavior than Hollywood and big media:

A study by the University of California at San Francisco Medical School of the films that generated over ninety-nine percent of American box office revenues from 1999 to 2003 found that eighty percent depicted smoking, a level not seen since the 1950s.[451] A Dartmouth Medical School study published in 2003 analyzed the film viewing habits of twenty-six hundred nonsmoking adolescents. It found that those whose exposure to smoking in films was in the highest twenty-five percent were nearly three times more likely to smoke two years later than those whose viewing habits put them in the lowest quarter of exposure to movie smoking. After evaluating the influence of other factors, the researchers concluded that exposure to *movie smoking was a greater influence on those who began smoking than all other causes combined.* The effect was even more pronounced on children whose parents did not smoke.[452] The San Francisco researchers used their data and the Dartmouth study to conclude that smoking in films causes 390,000 American children to begin smoking each year.[453]

It might seem pointless for government to try to compete against the behavioral influence of the film industry, with its annual box office revenue of thirty-four billion dollars,[454] or the tobacco industry, with its eleven billion dollar annual expenditure on promotion and advertising.[455] However, several states spend hundreds of millions of taxpayers' dollars each year on prime-time television commercials in an effort to dissuade people from smoking.[456] The good news is that this effort seems to work,[457] especially in California, which has one of the longest and most aggressive campaigns. In 1988, the average adult Californian annually smoked about eighty percent of the number of cigarettes that an adult did in the rest of the U.S., but in 2006 the average adult Californian smoked just half as many. This is all the more remarkable because while the inflation adjusted cost of the State's anti-smoking efforts increased by just ten percent from 1990 to 2003, the tobacco industry's promotional expenditures increased by more than four hundred and sixty percent.[458]

Good news? Yes. Can it work for gender equality? Yes, but as with any good ad campaign, targeting is important. For instance, in the California anti-smoking campaigns that targeted teens, different ads had different success rates. What didn't work were campaigns that lectured teens or stressed how smoking would harm their health.[459] You can probably guess why. Teens tend to believe they are invulnerable,[460] and ignore messages from their parents and other authority figures.[461]

Which messages did work? If you've ever thought much about the content of television ads for clothes or cars, you probably already know the answer: consumers' desires to be more admired by others are very powerful motivators. The most effective ads for reducing teenagers' interest in smoking showed smokers as foolish or unpopular. In one experiment, 1667 seventh and tenth graders were divided into groups, and each group watched one of eight video tapes of commercials centered on a particular anti-smoking theme. Each individual then completed a questionnaire designed to measure his or her behavioral intentions. The only themes with significant impact were those emphasizing "that smoking poses severe social disapproval risks."[462] Once California figured this out, the rate of smoking by twelve to seventeen year olds fell by forty-seven percent from 1997 to 2001. Ten percent of middle school students in the U.S. smoked in 2002, but in California, just over four percent did.

Here are a few ideas – but not by any means an exhaustive list – for media campaigns.

❏   *Influencing girls and young women*

In spite of egalitarian changes made in some societies, gender power remains very unequal worldwide. (As the fifty-five cultures study observed, feelings of powerlessness contribute to neuroticism.[463]) In order to begin a dialog in which women can best assert their viewpoints and values, shouldn't they feel that their voices will be respected and heard? Part of attaining that respect involves raising some women's self esteem, which would bring other benefits, as well. An example of an ad campaign for that purpose could address a huge problem that I've seen every day in my work representing foster children: women whose fear or inexperience allows them to be drawn into abusive romantic relationships, putting themselves and their children at risk. Many women who become involved with illegal drugs and criminal activity report being led astray by boyfriends or husbands. These women may assume that female subordination is natural because of male dominance. In short, they believe that women *are* what men *do to them*.[464]

Girls and young women should be immersed in contemporary messages – with minimal moralism – showing the social pitfalls of becoming romantically involved with and having the children of men who do not respect them. Young people often have strong reactions to how they think their peers view them. Madison Avenue surely can design a comprehensive campaign showing girls and young women that certain self-protective behaviors can make them more respected by their peers, while other paths ultimately put their social standing at risk. Some of the content might include girls getting peer respect for leaving unhealthy relationships, walking away from unprotected casual sex (far more effective than an abstinence message), or attaining financial self-sufficiency before getting themselves attached and pregnant.

Many girls are not getting the message that anything is possible. They understand that the vast majority of wealth and influence is in the hands of men. Another campaign could tell the stories of how some women who are not celebrities have attained respect, independence, influence and life satisfaction.

It may be unrealistic to expect that men seeing this campaign would change their disrespectful or unhealthy behavior in response. If more women were motivated to find and manage healthy relationships, however, men's behavior probably would improve as women's expectations increase – at least in developed countries where women have basic rights.

❏   *Influencing boys and young men*

The campaign just described would help address Susan Faludi's question, "why so many women 'choose' abusive men."[465] A campaign altering men's expectations is the other part of the equation for progress – in order to change the answer to Faludi's second question, why "there are so many abusive men to choose from."[466] This campaign could focus on violence and be directed toward children, and the parents and educators who are training them.

Some of the largest companies in the world encourage intimate partner battering though their record labels that sell rap and heavy metal music promoting misogynist violence and sexual exploitation. This music pervades the world of many teenagers, makes abuse seem normal to young people, and reinforces the inferiority and fear felt by many young women. One ad series could play misogynist music along with shots of people enjoying it, but then reacting in disgust when supertitles showing the lyrics appear on screen. The wives of male sports and entertainment celebrities could urge them to do spots describing why domestic violence is wrong.

We have to make it easier for boys to be more *empathetic* toward others and more inclined toward compassion and cooperation rather than conflict and violence. A part of that process is to reduce the influence of bullying. Timothy McVeigh's story is chilling. He was bullied as a boy. As an adult, he retaliated against the biggest bully he could find – the U.S. government. In 1995 he blew up the Murrah Federal Building in Oklahoma City, killing 168 people.[467] Exactly four years and one day later, two teenage boys shot themselves and thirteen classmates in Columbine, Colorado. A study of all twenty-eight U.S. school shootings between 1993 and 2002 revealed that all of the shooters were male and all were bullied prior to the shootings.[468] On any given day, sixty percent of teenagers in America see one or more incidents of bullying.[469] In the year after 9/11, a survey showed that the terrorist threat most feared by teens was bullying, not attacks by America's enemies.[470]

Decreasing violence in schools or on city streets requires reducing interpersonal tensions and provocations, and helping young men empathize with others. Antismoking efforts have demonstrated that effective advertising appeals to social standing by encouraging the belief that certain favored behaviors will enhance standing while disfavored ones will reduce it.

Many parents, schools and organizations are already working to reduce violence and increase empathy. Classroom programs focused on building empathy include the Character Education Partnership, the Knowledge Is Power Program, and Second Step: Student Success Through Prevention, Roots of Empathy.[471] Roots of Empathy, based in Canada, is remarkable in its success in utilizing infants to develop empathy in kids toward those less powerful than themselves. With money raised by an anti-domestic violence association for men called *Founding Fathers*, the *Family Violence Prevention Fund* created television advertisements that urge men to teach boys "that violence has no place in a relationship."[472] Norway introduced a comprehensive anti-bullying program that cut the incidence in half in the first two years and kept it low thereafter.[473] All parents and schools should teach nonviolence and empathy, and web and television advertising campaigns should be a major part of the effort.

Could we feminize boys too much?	Hawks may claim that reducing boys' tendency to rely on conflict and violence might make their nation militarily vulnerable. In the United States, momism (excessive mothering) was blamed when some young men refused or were not able to fight in World War II.[474] According to legend, many French mothers were determined to eradicate war following the trench warfare that slogged across France for more than five years in World War One. By deliberately instilling pacifist thinking in a generation of French men who grew to fighting age in the late 1930s, the story goes, these mothers unwittingly caused France's defeat at the hands of the Germans early in the next world war. Criticism of French pacifism resurfaced in 2003, when France threatened to veto a proposed U.N. Security Council resolution authorizing the U.S. to invade Iraq.
	Is it true that pacifist mothering is to blame France's military defeat? Read two other theories and see what you think.

- France's fighting resolve was not substantially different from that of England, Poland and many other nations that withered under the German onslaught early in World War II. The German *blitzkrieg* military strategy overwhelmed and subdued all its adjacent neighbors, not only France. The main thing that saved England was the large body of water that separates it from Germany.

- Many historians place some of the blame for France's defeat on a huge strategic error made by its generals and political leaders whose boyhood was well before the alleged pacification after World War I. France built a series of massive fortifications along its border with Germany, and the Germans simply went around them via Belgium. The guns of the Maginot Line could only face east and the Germans overran them from the west. (If the French had employed some women defense planners, would their strategy have been less rigid?)

As paradox five described, girls bully, too. The Girls Leadership Institute is one of a number of twenty-first century organizations providing classes, programs and camps for building both girls' self-esteem and their skills in neutralizing bullies. Author Kelly Valen recommends focusing on educating mothers about the social messages they give their daughters.[475] As a kindergarten teacher observed, "The mean girls are often from mean moms."[476] An ad campaign to address that problem could show a mom driving her daughter to school and making disparaging comments about the appearance of other mothers and their daughters, followed by the child later repeating some of those comments in a demeaning manner to shamed classmates, followed those classmates tearfully repeating those insults to their horrified mothers. The tag line could be: "Think what you say can't turn your child into a bully?"

❑ *Influencing men*

Another goal could be to encourage men to be more aware of and sympathetic to women's circumstances, abilities and needs. Such men would be more inclined to support public policies addressing women's needs and political agendas, and individual women who seek positions of power in government and business. Helping men become more supportive is perhaps the key step in women attaining power and influence. And men who are supportive are the best ambassadors to persuade other men.[477]

Some examples of issues that ad campaigns could address:

- Workplace discrimination: women should be allowed to advocate for themselves as men do in the workplace. Reminiscent of the studies described in paradox four, spots could show examples of how men judge women unfairly for asserting themselves. For example, a man who protests getting undesirable assignments with his boss later saying, "he's learning to stand up for himself," could be contrasted with women being criticized behind their backs either for being not strong enough to work their way up the ladder or for being "aggressive bitches." The tag line, in a male voice, could be: "Is this boss you?"
- Part time work options: ads during the Sunday morning news shows could feature brief testimonials from women who left the workforce because they could not find less than full time work, combined with an onscreen rolling counter tallying their employers' loss of both the investment in training them and their accrued experience and wisdom. Some of the spots could feature male caregivers who have left their careers, noting that

this is not just a women's issue. The ads could conclude with a CEO of a company with great employee retention policies beaming at a shareholders meeting as he or she reports record earnings.

- Affordable quality childcare: Similar to the part time ads, testimonials from parents who can't find good childcare – and its effect on their careers and their children – could personalize the problem. Compelling photographs of the poor conditions some children face in daycare facilities could add to the appeal of the message. Just as above, the ads could conclude with a CEO of a company with great childcare policies beaming at a shareholders meeting as he or she reports record earnings.

Even if ads such as those described in this section ran ten times a day on all the major networks, they would still be a minority voice compared to all the consumer advertising linking beauty and wealth to happiness, and all the misogyny found in some popular music and videos. To be effective, the ads would have to very compelling. Advertising professionals could donate their time and combine their efforts to create great ads that can compete with what already floods the media.

Rewarding entrepreneurial and grass roots campaigns also should be a key part of changing attitudes. For example, the Dutch government created a "Modern Man Prize," and awarded it to one who created a campaign to encourage men to work part time schedules instead of full time.[478] Similar prizes and grants could recognize and assist other efforts to change attitudes about gender.

Margaret Mead said that it takes two generations to create lasting social change.[479] The first generation has to change their behavior and create a new social norm. Then the behavior has to be reinforced in their children. The campaigns should run for at least forty years, with periodic creation of new spots and formats over time. This duration would ensure its effect on the children of people who have been favorably influenced by the campaign. Some useful ideas have been described here, but others surely merit similar wide exposure.

Making Women's Rights Human Rights

One of the notions that most oppresses women is that women's basic rights are culturally conditional rather than universal. In some cultures, women and girls are not able to go to school, get medical care or leave their homes to be in the community. Women are assaulted or killed because of gender. Hillary Clinton, speaking as First Lady in 1995, declared that women's rights are human rights. But that was no more true in practice then, than it was more than fifteen years later when she was representing the U.S. as Secretary of State.

The universalist view could be cast in stone via international treaties. Paradox ten described the primary vehicle, the *United Nations Convention on the Elimination of All Forms of Discrimination against Women*. Although simply ratifying treaties does not automatically eliminate discrimination, it lays an important part of the foundation for the rest of the process.

One hurdle in making women's rights universal human rights is that as long as there are at least thirty-four male Republicans in the U.S. Senate, such treaties will never pass. If passage is important to a voter, it would make sense to vote for Republican women or Democrats in any senate race. There is no guarantee that every Republican woman and Democrat would support these treaties, but it's pretty clear that no male Republican will.

Taking it to the next level:	If Congress did want to push women's human rights a step further, it could enact a law barring foreign aid to any nation that by policy or inaction condones misogyny, including denial of medical care or education because of gender, or that fails to prosecute rape, honor killing, or gender-selective abortion and infanticide. Barred nations might include China, India, Pakistan and the fundamentalist Islamic nations columnist Nicholas Kristof called the "Axis of Medieval."[480]

The law could work in the same way as an existing ban on funding for nations that sponsor terrorism. The State Department would issue warnings at first and gradually ramp up to economic sanctions if changes did not occur. This anti-terrorism strategy has not worked on every nation, and some ignore it. But the case of Libya gives hope. Libya, an Islamic nation, was considered such a dangerous source of terrorism that the U.S. bombed it in 1986, and Libya retaliated by exploding a bomb in Pan Am Flight 103 over Scotland two years later. However, years of economic sanctions finally took their toll and Libya's President-for-life Muammar Gaddafi decided to end his nation's terrorist activities. The sanctions ended by formal agreement in 2008. (Gaddafi was killed in a civil war backed by NATO in 2011.) |

The Rape Project

The right to be free from rape presents systemic and multi-faceted problems. Because of AIDS, HIV and other sexually transmitted diseases, rape is a world-wide public health crisis. Moreover, rape denigrates women, fosters fear of men that contributes to women's subjugation, and brutally retards efforts toward gender equality. Rape may subject women to severe public stigma or even ostracism, and in places where abortion is not relatively available saddles them with children they probably don't want. In some Islamic nations, rape victims may be jailed, subjected to further assault or even killed.[481] Nearly one out of every five American women will be victims of rape or attempted rape in their lifetime.[482] The prevalence of rape in the U.S. military is an extremely serious problem, and also illustrates the extent to which rape is tolerated by civilian society.

The global community of nations has been slow to condemn rape in war. Military forces have used rape in countless conflicts as part of campaigns to terrorize, punish or drive out civilian populations. To cite just a few examples: in Bosnia – perpetrated by Serb troops against Muslims,[483] in Guatemala – by government troops against suspected rebel sympathizers,[484] by the Japanese during World War II, and in Darfur – by Arabs against "blacks."[485] The government of Burma used this "weapon of war" as recently as 2002 in attempting to quell an ethnic rebellion.[486] War crimes have been punished in international tribunals since 1946, but it was not until 1998 that mass rape was found to be a crime against humanity – by a tribunal in Rwanda.[487] The United Nations Security Council finally agreed on a resolution in 2008 condemning rape as "a tactic of war" that should be excluded from amnesty when conflict ends.[488] But in Congo, ground zero for rape as an instrument of war and where the armed conflagration has seen two million victims, enforcement remains elusive.[489]

National and world leaders could apply greater political capital and economic resources toward reducing the incidence of rape, especially through multilateral efforts. These efforts should target all forms of rape, including child sexual abuse, sexual slavery and trafficking, and wartime and prisoner rape, and incorporate both "carrot" motivations, such as funding, and "stick" penalties, such as sanctions.

Programs to reduce rape also could include domestic violence. Intimidation and violence directed against women foster rape by breaking women's will to resist. Domestic violence is a human rights violation, according to the 1995 United Nations Fourth World Conference on Women. Amnesty International went further in 2001, declaring domestic violence to be a form of torture. This assertion relied on the *U.N. Convention against Torture and Other Cruel, Inhuman or Degrading Treatment or Punishment*, an international treaty that bans infliction of severe pain or suffering intended to intimidate or coerce.[490] (Sadly, torture is not a platform from which the U.S. has the moral authority to rail against domestic violence.)

An international project could track the frequency of rape and domestic violence around the globe and point out cultural and governmental differences that contribute to higher rates in certain regions or countries. Goals could then be established and publicized, with special funds available to support innovative solutions. For example, in India violent harassment of women in public places by groups of men is euphemistically called "eve teasing."[491] In an effort to reduce the high rates of violence against women and rape in New Delhi, the state began a program in 2008 requiring school boys to annually sign a pledge to respect women. Eve Ensler, *The Vagina Monologues* playwright, started an effort in Congo to help rape victims become political leaders.[492]

Funding criteria should encourage prevention and exclude solutions that rely exclusively on harsh punishment. After a compliance period, countries that do not meet goals could face closer monitoring and sanctions. Where rape is a weapon of war, the United Nations Security Council should refer the leaders responsible to the International Criminal Court for indictment and prosecution. (Sadly, the U.S. does not participate in that court.)

Putting pressure on governments carries the risk that some countries would under-report rape and domestic violence. Any monitoring effort should survey the population in order to compare actual incidence with reported crime statistics. A stumbling block for United States participation in such a program could be fear of international monitoring of the deplorable conditions in U.S. prisons, especially the incidence of prisoner rape.[493]

A mind can be a difficult thing to change. Two important steps in changing public perceptions are persuasion and formalizing shared understandings. If within two generations we want to achieve a society in which women's equality is the norm, the advertising and public relations campaigns described here are likely essential – as is creating shared understandings about the universality of that equality.

Chapter 14. Resolving the Paradoxes with Public Policy Changes

"[F]eminists struggle against any social, racial, economic, or physical abuse that threatens women's capacity to work and to love." Sara Ruddick[494]

Most readers probably agree with the goals stated in the previous two chapters, even if they have reservations about how best to achieve them. What lies ahead could be more problematic for some, because it may contradict their political beliefs concerning their core social and economic values. As a student of both, it seems clear to me that people often compromise their political social beliefs on the altar of their economic values or self interest. The reverse is also true, especially for political conservatives, because of a response to what economists call the "free rider effect." Conservatives tend to place high or even extreme importance on ensuring that others they perceive as having different moral values than their own are not getting an undeserved reward for little or no effort – especially if that reward flows though government using public tax dollars. Perceived free riders can and often do profoundly offend conservatives' moral sense of community, public order and cultural traditions.[495] The intense objections of some medically uninsured or uninsurable conservatives to President Obama's 2010 national health care plan, despite its probable benefits to them personally, illustrated the depth of this reaction.

This book will not likely convince passionate conservatives to abandon their rejection of social safety nets they call "socialism."

But those who place also high importance on women's greater political and economic influence may want to reassess their basic assumptions about government's role in social welfare after looking at that role through the lens of gender. As described in the next section, the same may be true regarding national security policies.

If we changed the values of our society so that the right to basic human needs became a preeminent value, more societal assets would be invested to help families and increase children's chances of growing into productive citizens. Women's leadership skills and priorities would become more important, because compared to men, women legislators have greater concern for the needs of families.[496] It's no coincidence that many of the nations choosing to have the highest social safety nets also have the most women in positions of power and influence. (They also tend to have more homogeneous societies than the U.S., and, prior to some recent strife over immigration, less discord about perceived free riders.) Humanitarianism seems to have especially benefitted women and women's efforts to lead.

Another illustration of women's societal values is found in the bank started by Nobel Peace Prize winner Muhammad Yunus, which along with a rapidly growing number of other micro finance organizations, makes small loans to poor people in developing countries. By design ninety-six percent of Grameen Bank's customers are women, in part because they are more likely than men to take care of their children with the profits from businesses they start. They also are more likely to invest in viable business ventures and pay back the loans. Yunus observes that, in contrast to men, women "have a longer vision."[497] This also is true in the U.S., where women are better at long term investing than men,[498] making women's skills more valued when the focus is on generational investing.

Second Bill of Rights

President Franklin Roosevelt described a set of principles for ensuring all people have the basic necessities of life in his 1944 State of the Union Address that he called the *Second Bill of Rights*. Law Professor Cass Sunstein wrote about it in 2004,[499] and Michael Moore featured lost film footage of the address in his 2009 film, *Capitalism: A Love Story*. The short version is this:

- A job with a living wage
- Business freedom from unfair competition and monopolies
- A decent home
- Medical care
- Education

But what might the *Second Bill of Rights* mean in practice? It could mean reinstituting some New Deal era job engines such as the Work Projects Administration and the Civilian Conservation Corps when unemployment rises above a certain threshold. Today's official measurement of unemployment includes little more than half of those unemployed. It does not include persons who are not actively seeking work, including those who have become discouraged because of lack of opportunities. A society guaranteeing a job with a living wage would want to include those discouraged people in its measure of and response to unemployment. A commitment to a living wage should include a minimum wage attuned to the cost of living in each region. Business freedom could be enhanced by more vigorous enforcement of existing anti-monopoly and unfair competition laws.

The right to a decent home could mean greater efforts to get people off the streets, out of temporary shelters and into safe long-term housing. It could also mean greater protection from predatory lending practices so that people who own homes would not lose them. A commitment to medical care for all could mean that citizenship would convey the right to see a doctor for preventative care, not just charity crisis care in an emergency room. An educational right could mean financing public schools in ways so that poor communities would not have inferior schools. It could also mean that financial hardship would not prevent young people from attending a community college or trade school, and that no one would have to borrow more than what they could expect to earn in their first year after graduation in order to attend a public university.

Political philosopher John Rawls created a rationale for such social safety nets in his landmark book, *A Theory of Justice*. He proposed morally optimizing social and political structures by having people imagine themselves shielded by a "veil of ignorance" from knowledge about their place in society, and then building institutions, laws and policy as if they might find themselves at any socioeconomic level. After imagining a Rawls' veil of ignorance about one's socioeconomic standing in society, a natural consequence is wanting to set a decent floor on which the lowest would stand.

Rawls' veil is also a test. If applying the veil to a particular identifying characteristic such as race, height or gender produces a different social or political structure than the status quo, it suggests that the existing structure is unjust. Taking gender as an example, if men had built our societies not knowing which gender they would be within those societies, our societies most certainly would be different than they are. The test demonstrates that addressing inequities that result from gender is essential to achieving justice in public policy, and that Rawls' veil should include ignorance about which gender one would be in a planned society.[bb]

Admittedly, getting people to care about others enough to devote more public resources to help them is not an easy value to instill in politics. There was great enthusiasm for Bush's sweeping tax cuts in 2001, largely drowning out voices fearing that this would cause the national debt to mushroom. Yet at the end of the decade, concerns about the national debt become the spearhead for opposition to economic stimulus and safety net spending. The last U.S. President to preach about the evils of greed and exploitation, Jimmy Carter, was voted out of office after a single term – the first to suffer that fate since the start of the Great Depression.

For nearly a hundred years political conservatives have complained about creeping socialism and preached that it would crush the lust for wealth and the wild abandon of unbridled capitalism, thus stalling the engine of our miraculous economy. But the fact that unrestrained speculation caused the 2008 worldwide economic collapse suggests that we could do better with less reckless greed.

The Introduction referred to the nations of Finland, Iceland, Norway, New Zealand and Sweden ("FINNZS") as models for women's progress.[500] Embracing their social safety net approach does not require becoming economically unsustainable PIIGS (Portugal, Ireland, Italy, Greece and Spain). We can make

---

bb. Professor Drucilla Cornell created the concept of the "imaginary domain," a psychic and moral space in which individuals can explore their own sources of happiness. Using this concept she variously argues that in the Rawlsian construct, women's perspective must be included in formulating a just societal framework, and that the imaginary domain must be a part of any just societal framework so as to ensure that the freedom of self actualization is available to all. Thurschwell at 44-51 (citing Cornell, THE IMAGINARY DOMAIN & AT THE HEART OF FREEDOM).

different choices and still live within our means. The collapse of
Iceland's unregulated banks in 2008's Great Recession came not
from Iceland's finance system being too much like the other
FINNZS, but instead from it being too much like the U.S.

It is doubtful that there is currently political support adequate to
build greater social safety nets based on the promise that they
would help more women rise to leadership positions in
government. Many citizens vote as if they believe that a society
driven by Ayn Rand's style of capitalism is the better path for the
U.S. But there is no evidence that in such a society the percentage
of women leaders in government and business would increase.[501]
Comparing the two major political parties in the U.S., the one
that is friendlier to European style socialism has substantially
more than twice as many women in state legislatures and
Congress – both in numbers and percentages – than the one that
rails against such socialism. Political conservatives often are
unfriendly to systematic attempts to expand women's
participation in leadership.

The U.S. may not be able to substantially increase opportunities
for women to have greater influence in society until it is willing
to follow the lead of countries where women have the most
influence. There does not appear to be the political will to
implement the public policy changes that would take us on this
path, which helps explain the plateaus and glass ceilings in the
new century described in the first paradox.

Working for Peace

Increasing opportunities for women in national and international
political leadership positions requires working to reduce the risk
of war. This is necessary because many of the people who oppose
female leadership also agree with Francis Fukuyama's assertion
that women leaders "would be less prone to conflict and more
cooperative" than men. Their fear, according to neoconservative

Fukuyama, is that there will remain other "parts of the world run by young, ambitious, unconstrained men" inclined to use violence, and that women leaders would be less likely than men to use the force necessary to stop them.[502] Many voters want men in charge when war threatens. A permanent state of war against terrorists and other enemies of the state decreases the importance of the women's movement to the mainstream public, as the aftermath of 9/11 demonstrated. Reducing the public's fear of war, however, could increase the appeal of female leadership.

It's no coincidence that many of the least militaristic nations also have the most women in positions of power and influence – places such as Iceland, Finland, Norway, Sweden, and Costa Rica. An example of how peace encourages women's leadership is found in New Zealand. Located in the South Pacific thousands of miles away from anywhere (except Australia), it does not possess significant reserves of oil, gold or other minerals that elsewhere have fueled greed and war. The threat of war in New Zealand is as remote as its location. In 2001, the government announced it was selling or retiring its entire fleet of fighter jets; they just seemed irrelevant. New Zealanders' choices for Prime Minister, opposition leader in Parliament, Governor-General, Chief Justice and Attorney General were all women. Any nation that increases its emphasis on peace would be more likely to elect women leaders.

In the U.S., the peace movement seems to have been largely subsumed by 9/11. Until it becomes a more potent political force, women's greater participation in government may remain a dream.

Equal Marriage

Rights for lesbian, gay, bisexual and trans-gender (LGBT) persons also are human rights. Not the least of these rights are those that pertain to marriage. These are very important to lesbians who want to marry, and also important to women's rights for another reason. A key step in increasing women's power and influence is transforming marriage. Decoding social gender roles and eliminating their unfair limitations on individual potential can't happen just from changes in the workplace and schools. Some of the old rules for marriages and relationships have to change.

Gay marriage is an unprecedented opportunity for such change. The religious right has this all wrong. Instead of threatening heterosexual marriage, gay marriage will strengthen it. Many LGBT couples are creating committed, mutually satisfying relationships without all of the Mars/Venus role stereotypes that have defined heterosexual marriage for thousands of years.[503] LGBT couples will be taking on a lot of personal challenges in this process, but what they learn will help everyone find greater equality in marriage, and thus help make the institution of marriage work for more women in the twenty-first century and beyond. This change will help more heterosexual couples bond and stay together as gender equality becomes reality, and in turn will help reduce the effects of negative gender stereotypes in society and the workplace. As more states join Massachusetts, Connecticut, Iowa, Vermont, New Hampshire and New York, and more countries join The Netherlands, Belgium, Spain, Canada, South Africa, Norway, Sweden and Argentina in legalizing gay marriage, they will gain a societal advantage. But until a majority of states have done so, it seems unlikely that the U.S. will be ready to embrace true social equality for women.

We could achieve equality for women without the broad social values described here, but it is unlikely we will do so. Feminism's failure to advocate effectively for such values helps explain the stalled progress in advancing women's equality, and women's full participation in political leadership.

Chapter 15. Resolving Some of the Paradoxes with Quotas

"When there are enough women in the room so that everyone stops counting, women become free to act like women."
Dee Dee Myers[504]

T he U.S. government has made efforts to remedy past discrimination, such as requiring women's athletics in schools to have the same resources as men's, and banning gender discrimination in hiring. The Democratic Party requires that women comprise at least half the delegates to its national convention. But the percentages of women in power in government and business still are dismal.

Our efforts to eliminate barriers to opportunity have not enabled women to close the gender gap. As noted in the second paradox, efforts toward equal opportunity in many ways seem to have benefitted men more than women. If it is desirable to put more women in leadership positions, this final suggestion would directly change political institutions in order to put more women in leadership positions. Unlike the suggestions in the previous three chapters, this one does not have any intrinsic value of its own. Its purpose is simply to help women advance. But it might backfire if women are not already empowered to lead on their own terms. As such, it should be considered a last resort – a final step to push things forward if the measures described in the previous chapter have been implemented and women's participation in legislatures needs a jumpstart.

Twenty-six Percent Rule

❏ *Background*

In comparison with many other democracies, the U.S. is far behind in women's participation in elective office. A substantial majority of the world's democracies reserve a percentage of seats for women in their legislatures and local policy-making bodies. Ironically, laws created under U.S. supervision in Afghanistan and Iraq require that twenty-five percent of their national legislators be women – significantly higher than American women's representation in Congress.[505]

Assessing the merits of gender quotas for legislatures is another chicken and egg problem. Does adding more women by quota change the priorities of a legislature? Excluding the quotas imposed by an outside army such as in Iraq and Afghanistan, it may be that most of these quotas are simply a marker of national acceptance of the legitimacy of women's voices in economic and political issues. Perhaps societies that adopt such quotas already are poised to adopt the values that women bring to public policy, and policy changes ascribed to women having been added to legislatures would otherwise have happened anyway in the absence of such quotas. While it's true that women legislators tend to focus more on family issues,[506] it is unknown if women added by quota significantly increase the success of this agenda.

Quotas may not necessarily change the paradigm for several reasons, not the least of which is that men usually continue to select the candidates. Men often choose tokens – women who are social males, or at the very least, loyal to the values of their sponsors. In Iraq, that has meant most women legislators espouse the positions of the men heading their tribes or religious sects.[507] Quota pressures increase the opportunity for nepotism, where retiring male officeholders may pick their inexperienced daughters or wives to replace them. Another problem is that quotas for rank and file legislators may take some time to affect men's retention of legislative and executive branch leadership positions from which they set the rules, and groom and pick their replacements.[508] And, women that have come up through a legislature's long standing traditions may not be quick to change priorities and procedures even when their numbers give them the power to do so.

A quota expands the pipeline, and in theory creates a greater flow of candidates toward higher leadership positions. But a quota that simply adds tokens to that pipeline may dilute the flow by lowering public expectation that women are agents of change. If voters do not believe that women candidates bring any unique benefits to public office, it may be harder for women who are real change agents to gain traction with the electorate. This in turn will increase the chances that women who rise to the highest leadership positions will be social males. If these pipeline disadvantages exist, care must be taken that they don't outweigh the advantages of whatever changes more women added by quota would bring to policy making.

Finally, as described in the critical mass paradox, using a quota to give women as much as half of the seats in a legislature does not necessarily bring women's values to the forefront. Rwanda's quotas were part of reforms instituted after the genocide that decimated roughly ten percent of its population in 1994. But in spite of Rwandan women attaining a majority in the national legislature in 2008, Rwanda remained a key combatant in the war that for ten years had been destroying neighboring Congo particularly by raping and mutilating its women.[509]

If it became clearer that increasing the numbers would significantly increase women's influence and change policies without women being coopted into the existing norms, then international efforts toward women's equality could be adapted to fit America's unique political system. Before explaining the mechanics of a way to do that using the twenty-six percent rule, here's a snapshot of the systems in some other democracies.

Over eighty countries, ranging from Argentina to India and most of Europe, have implemented various parliamentary quotas in order to increase women's representation.[510] Of the twenty nations in 2006 where women were over thirty percent of national legislators, eighty-five percent use gender quotas. Of the 102 nations with women more than ten but less than thirty percent of national legislatures, fifty-seven percent use quotas.[511]

In the 1990s, French women – who did not get the vote until 1944 – had the second lowest representation in elective office of any nation in Europe. Sylviane Agacinski, feminist scholar and wife of Prime Minister Lionel Jospin, led a campaign to remedy this.[512] In 1999, France enacted a plan requiring political parties to offer equal numbers of each gender on party list ballots for seats in local, national and European legislative bodies, or else lose public campaign financing. Although the smaller political parties embraced the idea, the largest parties were less enthusiastic.[cc] Nevertheless, the numbers of women in some elective offices and legislative bodies increased by more than eighty percent within three years after the plan took effect.[513] Spain joined the club in 2007, with a law requiring that each political party's candidate lists contain at least forty percent women.[514]

Costa Rica has a longer experience with a party list quota system, having enacted its law in 1988.[515] In 2006, Costa Rica had the largest proportion of women in a national legislature in the

---

cc. Sineau. Ironically, the party in greatest early compliance was the National Front, a far-right party that opposes abortion and believes women should stay at home and raise children. Murphy. But, National Front leader Jean-Marie Le Pen subsequently blamed his poor showing in the election on the parity law, complaining that "our score dropped because we had to present women of lower caliber than male candidates would have been." Bremner.

Western Hemisphere, at over thirty-eight percent, and ranked third in the world.[516] Perhaps Costa Rica's having abolished its army in 1948 made it easier for voters to trust women officeholders. Several surveys in 2009 listed Costa Ricans as the happiest people on earth.[517]

India amended its Constitution in 1993 to require that women be no less than a third of the members of its 265,000 panchayats. These village administrative agencies deliver services and resolve conflicts. Even though some women members are merely placeholders for their male relatives, a study concluded that panchayats headed by women delivered more public services than those led by men. In five Indian states, at least half the members of panchayats have to be women, and the federal government wants this rule extended to all states. As of 2011, a bill to create a similar quota in Parliament only passed the upper house.[518]

New Zealand is one of only three nations that raised the percentage of women in its national legislature to over thirty percent without a quota. A nation with pacifist leanings, it chose instead to establish a Ministry of Women's Affairs in 1986. This cabinet-level agency promotes laws and policies to raise the status of women. Perhaps more importantly, New Zealand had a head start on the rest of the world: in 1893 it was the first nation to grant women full suffrage.[519]

❑ *Mechanics and Impact*

If mentoring and training programs such as those described in the previous section were in place and the supply of mentored women capable of being change agents exceeded the demand of the political system, a quota system might accelerate adoption of women's values by the political process.

Neither party list quotas nor quotas for a percentage of seats in legislatures would be feasible in the U.S. without major structural changes incorporating systems such as proportional representation or multi-member districts. Considering that most U.S. voters have no experience with such systems – rather, a long tradition of two parties and one representative per district – it seems unlikely that voters would approve such drastic changes in how they cast their ballots for legislators. (Perhaps multi-member districts or proportional representation – in which voters choose or rank parties and each party receives a share of the seats in government proportionate to the share of votes it receives – could find more traction in local governments.)

A viable system that would not affect the mechanism by which individual voters cast their ballots would instead amend state constitutions to require that at least half the majority support needed for passing a bill in each chamber of the legislature come from women legislators. In other words, a block of women legislators equal to just over a quarter of the total seats in that chamber of the legislature would have to vote in favor of a measure for it to pass. This is the *twenty-six percent rule*. (The math is easy: only two states have lower houses so large that twenty-five percent plus one vote does not round to at least twenty-six percent.) If the political party or coalition in power did not have enough female votes to enact a bill from within its ranks, it would have to recruit those female votes from members of the other party.

Why base the rule on a majority? If it's unclear what percentage would constitute critical mass for substantial change, why not pick thirty percent, or sixty-five percent? Because women make up just over half of the adult population and of those who vote, in fairness a majority seems like the easiest ratio to justify to all voters.

Several specific provisions would make the rule fair and effective:

- Presently in most state legislatures such a rule could bring business to a halt, because the *total* number of female members is less than twenty-six percent. To get around this problem, the rule would start at a percentage of just above half of the current percentage of female representation in each chamber of a legislature. In legislatures where women's representation is near the national average of twenty-four percent, the rule could begin by requiring that women cast one-quarter of the votes needed to pass, or thirteen percent of the total seats. In a few states, because of the higher percentage of women in the party in power, the rule would have to be introduced at a percentage greater than half the current percentage of female representation in order to be effective.

- Staying ahead of the actual percentage of female legislators like the proverbial carrot on a stick, the rule would be set *on a one-way ratchet* and incrementally increases toward twenty-six percent as the percentage of women in each chamber rises toward parity with men. (In case of precipitous backsliding, there would have to be a failsafe provision that the rule percentage would always have to be less than the total percentage of women in a legislative chamber.)

- Women's gains in an election would not trigger a corresponding increase in the rule percentage until after the next election two years later. If women's gains came from the party in power, this delay might provide that party with a temporary respite from the effects of the rule – a reward for its efforts. If women's gains came from the party *not* in power, the delay would allow the majority party a chance to redouble its efforts before facing the consequences of a rule percentage increase. (The importance of going slow is illustrated by Norway's experience with board director quotas, described in paradox six, where a high quota probably was mandated too quickly.[520])

- In order to keep the rule relevant, an automatic failsafe provision would increase the percentage by one point if it had not yet reached twenty-six and had been too low to affect the party in power after the two most recent elections. In other words, if the party in power has within its ranks the female votes it needs to pass legislation under the rule for two election cycles, the percentage requirement would go up. Put yet another way, the rule percentage would grow automatically if it is lower than the percentage of women in a legislative chamber who are members of the majority party.

- The rule would not expire until at least ten years after the percentage of women in the state legislature reached fifty-one. The ten-year provision would prevent a temporary spike in women's representation from prematurely eliminating the rule.

Some important benefits of the twenty-six percent rule deserve more explanation. The rule could motivate the majority political party in a legislature to try to obtain a sufficient number of female representatives so as to be able to pass legislation on its own. The minority party would have the same motivation in positioning itself to assume the position of majority party.[dd] Thus, each party would likely recruit more female candidates and thus increase the number of women in elective office. Examples of how the rule could work in practice can be found at www.26percentrule.com.

Many of the women in Congress wear red jackets when they want to show solidarity. Its national colors are red, white and blue, but the U.S. still is only halfway to the day when the red jackets are even a third of the Congress. An additional consequence of

---

dd. There is a possibility that the members of the minority party would ignore the rule if they thought their party had no realistic chance to become the state's majority party.

growth in women's representation in state legislatures would be an increase in the pool of politically experienced women able to vie for seats in the U.S. Congress.

In part due to Republican gains in state races in 2002 and 2010, the percentage of women in state legislatures has remained stuck at twenty-three percent since 1999. In recent years there have been about twice as many Democratic women in state legislatures as Republican women, but this ratio has fluctuated with shifts in party power. In 2009 seventy-one percent of women state legislators were Democrats, and only sixty-one percent were in 2011.[521] The rule would make boosting the number of women of particular importance to the Republican party because it is so far behind its rival. (For example, women were twenty-four percent of Democrats in the U.S. House of Representatives in 2011, but only ten percent of Republicans. There were twelve female Democratic Senators, and only five Republicans.)

Another potential benefit from the rule relates to the discipline of the American two-party system that presently does not encourage legislators to form cross-party coalitions on issues. Politicians by necessity usually are loyal to party above all else. Party support and funding for reelection, for committee assignments and for a member's bills depend on his or her loyalty. By making it more necessary for proponents of legislation to solicit support from women *across the aisle*, women could be more empowered to create their own cross-party connections and policy agendas. Some party imposed hurdles to such cooperation might be lowered. Nations where women have crossed party lines to form powerful coalitions include Egypt, France, the Netherlands, Russia, Rwanda, South Africa and Sweden.[522] In Iraq, an assessment in 2008 said that women in the U.S. created parliament "are quicker to put aside sectarian differences."[523]

The rule also could increase the power and influence of women in the party not in power, because their votes would be needed to pass bills. Women who are minority party moderates supporting positions closest to the intersection the two parties' policy agendas might have the greatest voice when the party in power sought their support. In early 2009, the U.S. stood in the depths of one of the worst recessions in history. When the Democrats in the Senate needed three votes to pass an eight hundred billion dollar economic stimulus package, they made major changes in order to get the votes of two Republican women. This was all the more remarkable because these two were half of the Republican Party's female Senators. These women had more influence over that momentous legislation than anyone else in the nation.

The problem of leadership:	Women's presence in the most important seats of power in a legislature – the leadership elected by members – lags behind women's overall representation in legislatures. Again, the parties' ratios are quite different. In 2007, women held over seventeen percent of all leadership positions in state legislatures – twenty-seven percent of Democratic positions and under seven percent of Republican.[524] By 2010, women held even less – only sixteen percent of such leadership positions. Of the twenty-seven women in the highest ranks in 2010 – Senate Presidents or House Speakers – only four were Republicans. Of fifteen Majority Leaders, only one was a Republican. While Democrats have a small percentage gap between overall gender representation and leadership positions, for Republicans, that gap is huge – with women in leadership positions at a percentage less than half that of their general representation in legislatures. By putting more women in legislatures, the twenty-six percent rule likely would increase the number of Democratic women in these leadership positions, because that party has kept the gap between membership and leadership small. It is much less certain what effect the twenty-six percent rule would have on Republican legislative leadership positions.

❏ *Enactment*

Perhaps the biggest question this proposal raises is how such a change empowering women could ever be enacted and implemented, given that men still run government. Another problem is partisanship – the political party in power in a legislature is unlikely to support a requirement that it must obtain support from at least one member of the other party in order to pass laws and budgets. And similarly the minority party would not likely be in support if it expected that it could be in power one day, especially if its percentages of women legislators were significantly less than those of the majority party.

Enacting the rule would be unrealistic at the federal level because a Constitutional amendment would require ratification by two-thirds of Congress and three-quarters of the States – a nearly insurmountable hurdle. However, in seventeen U.S. states, twelve of which are west of the Mississippi, a ballot initiative passed by just a majority of those voting could accomplish it.[ee] In those states, legislative approval is not necessary. To paraphrase a popular song, sisters could do it for themselves. In the 2004 presidential election, fifty-two percent of the eligible voters and fifty-six percent of the actual voters were women. The effort could start by selecting one of these seventeen states and infusing substantial political organization and capital, just as George Soros did in using a voter initiative to reform the drug laws in California. (Ballot initiatives also are a way to implement several of the other suggestions in this book, including part time work, gay marriage, and the second bill of rights.)

Opponents might file lawsuits arguing that the twenty-six percent rule discriminates against men and violates the equal protection guarantee of the U.S. Constitution. But the courts do not

---

ee. www.citizensincharge.org/states. Four of those states also require that a particular percentage of voters voting in the election, ranging from thirty percent to a majority, actually vote yes on the proposed constitutional amendment. National Conference of State Legislatures, *Supermajority Vote Requirements*. The seventeen are: Arizona, Arkansas, California, Colorado, Illinois, Massachusetts, Michigan, Mississippi, Missouri, Montana, Nebraska, Nevada, North Dakota, Ohio, Oklahoma, Oregon and South Dakota.

scrutinize gender-based laws as rigorously as race-based laws,[525] and the U.S. Supreme Court sometimes has found remedial rules justified by some greater need such as correcting the effects of past discrimination. Despite its focus on states' rights, perhaps the present conservative Supreme Court would invalidate the twenty-six percent rule. But the resulting public discussion would raise awareness of the importance of women's equal representation in government.

Why wouldn't every underrepresented group deserve to have a variation of this quota scheme created for them? Women are entitled to a unique power guarantee for several reasons. First, they are the only subjugated group that *is a majority* in every town, region and nation – except in those nations that practice gender based abortion or infanticide, thus reducing the female population. Second, women's approaches to conflict resolution – influenced by both biology and socialization – are on average different from men's approaches and benefit everyone in society. Finally, unlike ethnic differences, there are some biological bases for women's different approaches to conflict resolution and policymaking.

Would the party in power thwart the rule by "buying off" a woman's vote from the other party?

The twenty-six percent rule would create more situations where votes in legislatures would be close because the majority party would need to get a female vote or two from the other side to pass bills. A party needing one vote to push forward its agenda may entice a turncoat from the other side to permanently join it by offering a choice committee chair assignment and other perks. The downside for the turncoat is that her former party may vilify her and work harder to defeat her at her next bid for re-election or election to higher office. That is why turncoats are rare. Enticement of a female turncoat could thwart the intent of the twenty-six percent rule, but the effect usually would last only through one election cycle due to the earlier described provision automatically increasing the percentage if it has had no effect.

The most famous recent examples of turncoats were men. Republican U.S. Senator Jim Jeffords changed party control of a split U.S. Senate in 2001 by declaring that he would become an independent and vote with the Democrats. In 2009, Republican Senator Arlen Specter switched parties and gave Democrats the sixtieth vote they needed to stop Republican filibusters. The effects of both of these turncoats' actions were short lived, undone by voters in subsequent elections. Specter's failed 2010 reelection bid illustrates the personal perils of switching sides.[526]

Dealing with independents and third parties:

In states with independent or third party legislators, the problem would be how to classify them. Probably the fairest system would specify that the votes of female third party or independent legislators who historically voted at least half the time with the particular party in power do not count toward fulfilling the necessary percentage set by the twenty-six percent rule. This is because the rule is intended to force the party in power to get more women elected, and to reach out to women across the aisle. Because she would not yet have a voting history by which to classify her, the vote of a newly elected independent woman legislator could count in reaching the rule percentages during her first two years in office.

Legislative chambers where the rule is moot:

All of the seventeen ballot initiative states would benefit from the rule's enactment, especially those where women's legislative participation remains stuck in single digit percentages. The good news is that among the seventeen states, the rule was not needed in three legislative chambers where women in the party in power in 2011 held more than half the number of seats needed to pass legislation. The State Senates of California, Massachusetts, Colorado and Oregon had attained the distinction of not needing the rule in the recent past, but by 2011 only the Massachusetts and Colorado Senates remained such strongholds. The Nevada and Colorado Houses also joined the club, but by 2011 the Nevada House stood alone. If enacted in Colorado, Massachusetts or Nevada, the rule might encourage the minority party in those legislative chambers where the rule was already met to work harder to increase the number of women legislators in their ranks in preparation for a return to power, in addition to directly spurring changes in those states' other legislative chambers. Not surprisingly, in all instances where women were a majority of legislators in the majority party, that party was the Democratic Party.

If we've gone as far as is practically possible with the changes suggested in the previous chapters and there are still states with poorly responding percentages of female state legislators, those states could raise their numbers with this variation on the method used by a large majority of the world's democracies.

Tokens

Although it is critical that we help more women attain positions of political power, and women need opportunities to stretch and grow, it is not helpful to put women in positions for which they are significantly underqualified. This is a concern at all levels of government, and of a particular importance where the twenty-six percent rule would put more pressure on political parties to increase the number of women legislators. Gender tokenism hurts the effort toward equality because if the public believes that women candidates often are not qualified for the positions they seek it encourages public complacency about women's underrepresentation in government. Even worse, a woman who attains an office beyond her capability and then performs poorly may block the pipeline for women for that office and similar ones for years to come by reinforcing old stereotypes about women's limitations.

Because women are underrepresented in politics, women candidates sometimes have less experience than their male opponents. Thus, it may be tempting for women candidates and their backers to adopt the political marketing strategy that experience and policy knowledge are not important. The next step down this path is that even when experienced women are available, a party may decide that a woman with qualifications, intellect and experience might be negatively regarded by many voters. A political party or organization may decide to put forward an under qualified woman candidate because of a belief that the average voter could better relate to her or at least would not feel intimidated by her.

It is insulting to women to think that just putting a woman on the ticket – no matter her positions on the issues or her qualifications

– will convince most women to vote for her, as *New York Times* op-ed columnist Gail Collins and many others complained about Republican vice presidential pick Sarah Palin in 2008.[527] However, feminist icon Gloria Steinem took Palin's candidacy as a compliment, saying, "You know what you're saying is important when the power structure brings in people who look like you and think like them."[528]

Conclusion: Using Gender Based Goals to Build a Better Future

By many measures women are better off today than they were forty years ago, and few women want to return to the social structure in place in the 1960's. However, feminism has not fulfilled its goals and has instead created many unresolved paradoxes. Given the causes and consequences of these paradoxes, how should we as a society plan for our future? Section Two of this book provides a range of options for readers and policymakers. Part time careers, more childcare and mentoring are in the first group. The second includes media campaigns, targeting rape and adopting and implementing a broader view of human rights. Next is setting national priorities of humanitarianism and peace, as well as recognizing the value of memes that flow from gay marriage rights. Finally, there is adopting the globally tested mechanism of legislative quotas. These suggestions certainly can't fix all of our problems related to gender, and you the reader is encouraged to put your creative ideas in play.

As I stated at the outset, it has not been my intention to make broad value judgments about gender. If the reader has concluded that I think women are better than men in some overall sense, then I may have failed to communicate what's behind this effort. I am not saying the world would be a better place simply if more women were in charge. (Even though I am guilty of making a value judgment about men's greater propensity toward violence and war.) There may be benefits in women's greater influence and power from diversity of viewpoint and experience, and societal fairness. But the point of this book is that if we create the conditions described in chapters twelve to fourteen that would lead to more women having more power and influence, those conditions – by themselves – also would make the world a better place.

In at least one way, I may have been too hard on feminism. By reviewing modern feminism's consequences roughly forty years after its genesis, I do not mean to suggest that it has failed because all the change it promised was not delivered within forty years. Forty years is simply the time that's elapsed so far, so it seems fair to point out the areas where change has been too agonizingly slow or has made things worse. But many of my suggestions may not be accomplished in forty years either. The effort needed for the entire process of shifting the social matrix seems overwhelming – a collective, continuous and committed effort for longer than the span of one lifetime.[529] That obstacle did not stop feminist visionaries Susan B. Anthony, Elizabeth Cady Stanton and Matilda Joslyn Gage, who knew they would never live to see the realization of their goal of women's suffrage. Gage wrote, "We are battling for the good of those who shall come after us; they, not ourselves, shall enter into the harvest."[530] The essence of civilization is building a better life for our descendants. That is the best investment of our political and social capital.

I invite you to ask, what would happen if we turned our thinking upside down and:

- Oprah gave all of her billions to journalist and women's rights crusader William Kristof to spend on projects to help women?

- Bill Gates announced that the other half of his foundations' billions not devoted to vaccines henceforth would go to projects to help women and girls?

- Every professional basketball player making over one million dollars a year made a public service spot against domestic violence or rape and paid to air it on TV shows aimed at the young male demographic?

- The U.S. ratified the international treaty banning gender discrimination, the *United Nations Convention on the Elimination of All Forms of Discrimination against Women* (CEDAW)?

- The Federal government and all companies and organizations receiving federal funds were required to offer flexible workplace policies and reduced schedules to all employees?

- The U.S. went from seventy-fourth in world rankings of women's percentages in national legislatures, where it is in the company of Albania and Turkmenistan, to fourth?

- The leaders of the world's most popular religions joined the Dalai Lama in declaring themselves to be feminists, and issued doctrinal and policy changes creating equality for women?

Call or write Oprah, Bill Gates, a pro basketball player, your elected representatives, your religious leaders, and other influential people and ask. If you don't get action, become influential yourself.

Appendix: Deleted Scenes

Earlier drafts of the book contained a section on mothers who abandon their children, and a chapter about bonobos, who don't. Those no longer have a place here. Although the two other sections that follow don't fit the flow of the narrative in the final version, they do amplify it.

Authors Rosalind Barnett and Caryl Rivers don't prove gender sameness in their book Same Difference.

In their book *Same Difference*, authors Rosalind Barnett and Caryl Rivers make numerous claims that men and women are the same that are not supported by the sources they cite. For example, they assert there are no differences in the ways male and female judges approach or perform their work. For support they quote only two sources. The first is a speech by U.S. Supreme Court Justice Sandra Day O'Connor in 1991 stating her personal views on judging. However, a speech by one justice, the first women ever appointed to the high court, is hardly, as they claim, a "debunking" of the notion that women judges speak with a " 'different voice.' "[531]

Their second source is a "major study" they say was published in the "*Indiana Law Review*" and from which they quote: " 'most female judges do not decide cases in a distinctly feminine or feminist manner.' "[532] Their "quotation" actually is a paraphrase and their citation refers not to the *Indiana Law Review*, but instead to an article in *The New Yorker*. Readers who take the trouble to find and read *The New Yorker* piece discover that the referenced law article appears in the *Indiana Law Journal*, a different publication from the *Law Review*.[533]

Barnett and Rivers misrepresent the nature and significance of the *Indiana Law Journal* article, which does not reach the definitive conclusion they claim. The *Indiana* article is described by *The New Yorker* piece as a "mostly anecdotal" study.[534] A section in the *Indiana* article entitled "Empirical Perspectives" lists only the following sources:

- studies, summarized in a single paragraph, analyzing the first wave of female judges in the 1970s and 80s – long before the big surge in the Clinton era of the 1990s;
- a review of the voting and opinions written by the two women justices on the U.S. Supreme Court during the 1993 term;
- essays and speeches written by some women judges on how they *believe* they approach judging; and,
- an analysis of *a sample* of published opinions written by the twenty-two female judges who sat on the United States Courts of Appeals from 1981 to 1990.[535] (The analysis actually found significant differences by gender in discrimination cases.)

Barnett and Rivers ignore the following honest assessments in *The New Yorker* article: The feminist judging "hypothesis has proved difficult to test. There is no practical way to provide male and female judges – especially trial-court judges, who work alone – with identical issues to resolve; moreover, it can be difficult to identify which result in a given case is more or less 'female.' "[536] Even the lead author of the Indiana article concedes that he could not disprove a feminine influence on judging. Interviewed in *The New Yorker* article, he admits his study only showed that " 'other parts of judges' backgrounds – like their party affiliation and their prior professional history – matter more than whether they are men or women.' "[537]

The *Indiana* article undermines Barnett and Rivers' assertion by concluding that while "the critical issue of whether men and women bring different perspectives to bear in their roles as judges … [remains] unsettled …, intuitive fairness justifies a goal of electing and appointing more women to the bench."[538] The article points out that even Justice O'Connor supports the goal that half of U.S. judges be women.[539]

The New Yorker piece highlights the difficulty in analyzing the role of gender in judging: teasing out all of the other personal factors that influence judges' decisions. The focus of the article is why Harris County, Texas is *not* a good laboratory for determining if women judges are more compassionate, even though in 2000 a majority of its judges were women. If the county, which includes Houston and suburbs, were a state it would rank third in the U.S. in the imposition of capital punishment. The article explains the political factors ensuring that only members of the most conservative segment of the legal community become judges in this county. It also profiles the most conservative member of the Texas Court of Criminal Appeals, a woman whose family fortune largely financed her election campaign.[540]

A large scale study of judging published in 2005, the year after Barnett and Rivers' book, succeeds in eliminating factors other than gender. Looking at the 556 sexual harassment and gender discrimination cases decided between 1999 and 2001 by three judge panels of the federal courts of appeals, it concludes that judicial gender matters a lot when what's at issue in a case is gender.[541] The study teases out factors such as age, length of time on the bench and prior employment history by showing that analyzing the data using those factors did not change the results. The author accounts for numerous design flaws of previous studies, including the analysis problem that Democrats tend to side more with plaintiffs and appoint more women – women who also are more sympathetic to plaintiffs – than do Republicans.[542]

Individual female judges side with plaintiffs in sexual harassment cases nearly twice as often as male judges, and are two-thirds more likely to do so in gender discrimination cases.[543] The more significant finding is that female Republican appointees side with sexual harassment and gender discrimination plaintiffs just as often as male Democratic appointees, in spite of the fact that Democratic judicial appointees generally are more favorable to discrimination plaintiffs than Republican appointees.[544]

And just as important is the impact female judges have on the votes of their brethren. Plaintiffs prevailed in only seventeen percent of the cases where there were no women on the panel, but thirty-four percent – twice as often – where a single female judge was present.[545] On the few panels where two women constituted a majority, forty three percent found for the plaintiff, but this was only due to the extra female vote. A second female judge had no additional impact on votes of male judges.[546] (Ironically, the sole case where the panel was all female went to the defendant.[547]) Having at least one woman on a panel more than doubles the likelihood of a ruling for the plaintiff in sexual harassment cases, and nearly triples it when gender discrimination is the issue. The more startling conclusion is that a female judge on the panel in such cases has a more than fifty percent greater effect on a male judge's vote than which party appointed that judge. Gender trumps ideology.[548]

The author of the study proposes a combination of several theories to explain the results, including that female judges persuade their male colleagues to view cases their way, male judges defer to female judges' experiences on some gender issues, the men offer support to the women on issues of importance to the women in the hope that women will reciprocate on some other issue in the future, or the mere presence of women causes men to be less extreme in their views[549] – what I call the anti-locker-room effect.

Putting more women on the bench is an important goal in a democracy. As Legislative Counsel for the California Judges Association for nearly six years, I had the privilege of working with many very competent and caring female judges. As in many fields not previously open to women, a few of the first women judges may have tried too hard to emulate the authoritarian style of some of their male colleagues. You'd be hard pressed to find anyone today who would argue that the growth in the number of women on the bench since the mid-1990s has had anything but a positive effect on the judicial system. In January 2010, twenty-eight percent of the active judges on the federal courts of appeals were women.

Whistle-blowers

The potential for significant social change from increases in women's power may be greater than at any time in history. *New York Times* columnist Maureen Dowd believes the post-Erin Brockovich era offers new hope for the future. Citing the role that women played in sounding the alarm about Enron's impending implosion, in 2002 she said:

> Only 10 years after Mattel put out Teen Talk Barbie whining "Math class is tough," we have women unearthing the Rosetta stone of this indecipherable scandal.
> ....
> It is men's worst fear, personally and professionally, that women will pin the sin on them, come "out of the night like a missile and destroy a man," as Alan Simpson said during the Hill-Thomas hearings.
> There has been speculation that women are more likely to be whistleblowers – or tattletales when they are little – because they are less likely to be members of the club.
> Some men suggest that women, with their vast experience with male blarney, are experts at calling guys

on it.

At Enron, it was men who came up with complex scams showing there was no limit to the question "How much is enough?" And it was women who raised the simple question, "Why?"[550]

Investigative journalist Marie Brenner agrees, "the women of Enron ... detected the web of intrigue, predicted the fall, [wrote] futile letters to board members, tipped financial analysts, and tried to avert the final collapse."[ff] The chief whistle-blower on the FBI's failure to prevent the 9/11 terrorist attacks was a career FBI Agent, Coleen Rowley.[551] *Time Magazine* named whistle-blowers Rowley, Sherron Watkins of Enron and Cynthia Cooper of Worldcom its "Persons of the Year 2002."[552] *Time* noted that having a husband's income to fall back on was not a source of their courage: all three are "the chief breadwinners in their families. Cooper and Rowley have husbands who are full-time, stay-at-home dads."[gg]

A theme of much writing about the phenomenon of female whistle-blowers is that in spite of women's professional ascension they are not encouraged, as men are, to self-identify as insiders. Whistle-blower Watkins observed, "Society doesn't ask women what you do for a living. Your ego or self-worth isn't [as] tied to what you do."[553] Some see women, outsiders in corporate and government culture, as "inherently 'disloyal to the civilization' " that depends on their labors.[554] Harvard Professor Barbara Reskin believes that women are free "to make moral

---

ff. Brenner at 184. However, a female attorney at accounting firm Arthur Andersen, Nancy Temple, played a key role in the Enron document shredding that led to Andersen's conviction for obstruction of justice and the firm's ultimate demise.

gg. Lacayo. Watkins did not intend to become a whistle-blower. A congressional committee obtained and then released her letter to Enron Chairman Kenneth Lay. *Id.*

decisions that people who are locked into a network have a hard time making."[555] By contrast, according to Watkins, most men identify as insiders and "have no friendships outside the workplace."[556]

These whistle-blowers, the new Paul Reveres, exemplify the themes Malcolm Gladwell describes in his book *The Tipping Point*: a small number of motived individuals with the right information and the right connections at the right time can stop the bad behavior of large institutions. The fear caused by whistle-blowers' actions inhibits financial fraud and institutional negligence, because those at the top cannot rely on their networks and institutions to protect them. Women whistle-blowers could be lurking around any corner. Writing about Rowley and Watkins, whistle-blower Anita Hill said, "the number of women in positions of authority is growing.... [So too] will their opportunities, not only to be whistle-blowers but, more important, to shape institutional standards from the top."[557]

Bibliography

10 Reasons the Battle of the Sexes is Over, TIME MAGAZINE, Mar. 8, 2010 (www.time.com/time/specials/packages/completelist/0,29569,1930277,00. html).

2001 Report of the Independent Auditor of the San Jose Police Department.

2005 Catalyst Census of Women Board Directors of the Fortune 500 (www.catalyst.org/file/9/2005%20wbd.pdf).

A guide to womenomics, ECONOMIST, Apr. 15, 2006, at 73 (www.economist.com/node/6802551).

Agacinski, Sylviane, PARITY OF THE SEXES (Lisa Walsh trans., Columbia Univ. 2001) (1998).

Amnesty International, *Afghanistan: Women still under attack – a systematic failure to protect* (May 30, 2005) (www.amnesty.org/en/library/info/ASA11/007/2005).

—— *Broken bodies, shattered minds – The torture of women worldwide* (Mar. 6, 2001) (www.amnesty.org/en/library/info/ACT40/001/2001).

Anderson, Jeffrey, *Firm Culture Still Hard on Families*, S.F. DAILY JOURNAL, Oct. 22, 2001, at 2.

Angier, Natalie, *Is War Our Biological Destiny?*, N.Y. TIMES, Nov. 11, 2003, at F1.

—— *Men, Women, Sex and Darwin*, N.Y. TIMES MAGAZINE, Feb. 21, 1999, at 48.

—— *No Time for Bullies: Baboons Retool Their Culture*, N.Y. TIMES, Apr. 13, 2004, at F1 (www.nytimes.com/2004/04/13/science/no-time-for-bullies-baboons-retool -their-culture.html?sec=&spon=&partner=permalink&exprod=permalink).

—— *Pay Gap Remains for Women in Life Sciences*, N.Y. TIMES, Oct. 16, 2001, at F3.

—— *Skipping Spouse to Spouse Isn't Just a Man's Game*, N.Y. TIMES, Sept. 1, 2009, at D2 (www.nytimes.com/2009/09/01/science/01angi.html).

Angier, Natalie, & Chang, Kenneth, *Gray Matter and the Sexes: Still a Scientific Gray Area*, N.Y. TIMES, Jan. 24, 2005, at A1.

Anomaly or Epidemic: the Incidence of Prisoner-on-prisoner Rape, in Human Rights Watch, *No Escape*, at 99-103 (news.findlaw.com/cnn/docs/hrw/hrwmalerape0401.pdf).

Archibold, Randal, *Octuplets, 6 Siblings, and Many Questions*, N.Y. TIMES, Feb. 4, 2009, at A14 (www.nytimes.com/2009/02/04/us/04octuplets.html).

Arnqvist, Göran & Rowe, Locke, SEXUAL CONFLICT (Princeton Univ. Press 2005).

Babcock, Linda, & Laschever, Sara, WOMEN DON'T ASK: NEGOTIATION AND THE GENDER DIVIDE (Princeton Univ. Press 2003).

Badkhen, Anna, *Liberation eludes Afghan women*, S.F. CHRONICLE, Apr. 16, 2004, at A1.

Badkhen, Anna & Haas, Danielle, *Women losing freedoms in chaos of postwar Iraq: Shiite clerics move into power vacuum*, S.F. CHRONICLE, May 24, 2002, at A1.

Baer, Judith A., OUR LIVES BEFORE THE LAW (Princeton Univ. Press 1999).

Ban leads call for greater efforts to end 'silent war' of sexual violence in conflict, UN DAILY NEWS, Jun. 19, 2008, at 1 (www.un.org/news/dh/pdf/english/2008/19062008.pdf).

Barnett, Rosalind & Rivers, Caryl, *Abu Ghraib Pulls 'Better Angels' Down to Earth*, WOMEN'S ENEWS, Sept. 1, 2004.

—— SAME DIFFERENCE: HOW GENDER MYTHS ARE HURTING OUR RELATIONSHIPS, OUR CHILDREN, AND OUR JOBS (Basic Books 2004).

Baron-Cohen, Simon, THE ESSENTIAL DIFFERENCE: THE TRUTH ABOUT THE MALE AND FEMALE BRAIN (Perseus Publishing 2003).

Batlan, Felice, *"If you become his second wife, you are a fool": Shifting paradigms of the roles, perceptions, and working conditions of legal secretaries in large law firms*, in Special Issue: Law Firms, Legal Culture, and Legal Practice, 52 STUDIES IN LAW, POLITICS AND SOCIETY 169-210 (2010).

Beauty and success: To those that have, shall be given, ECONOMIST, Jan. 4, 2008, at 53 (www.economist.com/node/10311266).

Belkin, Lisa, Blog, *Motherlode: Fired From the 'Mommy Track'*, N.Y. TIMES, Mar. 26, 2010 (http://parenting.blogs.nytimes.com/2010/03/26/fired-from-the-mommy-track).

—— *The New Gender Gap*, N.Y. TIMES MAGAZINE, Oct. 4, 2009, at 11 (www.nytimes.com/2009/10/04/magazine/04FOB-wwln-t.html).

—— *What's Good for the Kids*, N.Y. TIMES MAGAZINE, Nov. 8, 2009, at 9 (www.nytimes.com/2009/11/08/magazine/08fob-wwln-t.html).

Bennet, James, *Arab Woman's Path to Unlikely 'Martyrdom'*, N.Y. TIMES, Jan. 31, 2002, at A1.

Bennett, Jessica, *Generation Diva: How our obsession with beauty is changing our kids*, NEWSWEEK, Mar. 30, 2009 (www.newsweek.com/id/191247).

Bennhold, Katrin, *The Female Factor: 20 Years After Fall of Wall, Women of Former East Germany Thrive*, N.Y. TIMES, Oct. 5, 2010 (www.nytimes.com/2010/10/06/world/europe/06iht-letter.html).

—— *The Female Factor: Feminism of the Future Relies on Men*, N.Y. TIMES, Jun. 24, 2010 (www.nytimes.com/2010/06/23/world/europe/23iht-letter.html).

—— *The Female Factor: In Germany, a Tradition Falls, and Women Rise*, INT'L HERALD TRIB., Jan. 18, 2010 (www.nytimes.com/2010/01/18/world/europe/18iht-womenside.html).

—— *The Female Factor: In Sweden, Men Can Have It All*, N.Y. TIMES, Jun. 15, 2010, at A6 (www.nytimes.com/2010/06/10/world/europe/10iht-sweden.html).

—— *The Female Factor: Recession Seen Taking Toll on Gender Equality*, INT'L HERALD TRIB., Apr. 27, 2011 (www.nytimes.com/2011/04/27/world/europe/27iht-letter27.html).

—— *The Female Factor: Where Having It All Doesn't Mean Having Equality*, N.Y. TIMES, Oct. 12, 2010 at A4 (www.nytimes.com/2010/10/12/world/europe/12iht-fffrance.html).

—— *The Female Factor: Working (Part-Time) in the 21st Century*, N.Y. TIMES, Dec. 30, 2010, at A13 (www.nytimes.com/2010/12/30/world/europe/30iht-dutch30.html).

Bergner, Daniel, *What Do Women Want?*, N.Y. TIMES MAGAZINE, Jan. 25, 2009, at 26 (www.nytimes.com/2009/01/25/magazine/25desire-t.html).

Bernard, Tara Siegel & Lieber, Ron, *The High Price of Being a Gay Couple*, N.Y. TIMES, Oct. 3, 2009, at A1 (www.nytimes.com/2009/10/03/your-money/03money.html).

Bertrand, Marianne et al., *Dynamics of the Gender Gap for Young Professionals in the Financial and Corporate Sectors* (prepublication draft, Dec. 2009, for AMERICAN ECONOMIC JOURNAL: APPLIED ECONOMICS) (http://faculty.chicagobooth.edu/marianne.bertrand/research/dynamics_120 9.pdf).

Birkhead, Tim, PROMISCUITY: AN EVOLUTIONARY HISTORY OF SPERM COMPETITION (Harvard Univ. Press 2000).

Black, M.C. et al, *The National Intimate Partner and Sexual Violence Survey: 2010 Summary Report*, National Center for Injury Prevention and Control, Centers for Disease Control and Prevention (2011) (www.cdc.gov/ViolencePrevention/pdf/NISVS_Report2010-a.pdf).

Bonner, John Tyler, THE EVOLUTION OF CULTURE IN ANIMALS (Princeton Univ. Press 1980).

Boone, Jon, *'Worse than the Taliban' – new law rolls back rights for Afghan women*, GUARDIAN, Mar. 31 2009, at 1 (www.guardian.co.uk/world/2009/mar/31/hamid-karzai-afghanistan-law).

Boswell, John, THE KINDNESS OF STRANGERS: THE ABANDONMENT OF CHILDREN IN WESTERN EUROPE FROM LATE ANTIQUITY TO THE RENAISSANCE (Pantheon Books 1988).

Boushey, Heather, *Opting Out? The Effect of Children on Women's Employment in the United States*, 14 FEMINIST ECONOMICS 1 (2008).

Boustany, Nora, *Janjaweed Using Rape as 'Integral' Weapon in Darfur, Aid Group Says*, WASHINGTON POST, Jul. 3, 2007, at A9 (www.washingtonpost.com/wp-dyn/content/article/2007/07/02/AR200707 0201627.html).

Bower, Joseph & Christensen, Clayton, *Disruptive Technologies: Catching the Wave*, HARVARD BUSINESS REV., Jan.-Feb. 1995.

Boy, Angie & Kulczycki, Andrzej, *What We Know About Intimate Partner Violence in the Middle East and North Africa*, 14 VIOLENCE AGAINST WOMEN 53, 59-61 (2008).

Brashares, Justin S., *Ecological, behavioral and life-history correlates of mammal extinctions in West Africa*, 17 CONSERVATION BIOLOGY 733-43 (2003).

Braudy, Leo, FROM CHIVALRY TO TERRORISM: WAR AND THE CHANGING NATURE OF MASCULINITY (Knopf 2003).

Braw, Elisabeth, *Q&A with Madeline Albright: Brooching the subject of diplomacy*, METRO WORLD NEWS, Oct. 5, 2009 (www.teovan.com/news/2009/10/05/20091005055504001005-QA-with-M adeline-Albright--Brooching-the-subject-of-diplomacy.php).

Bremner, Charles, *Chirac on course for big parliamentary majority*, THE TIMES (London), Jun. 10, 2002, at 1.

Brenner, Marie, *The Enron Wars*, VANITY FAIR, Apr. 2002, at 180.

Brizendine, Louann, THE FEMALE BRAIN (Morgan Road Books 2006).

Brooks, Arthur, GROSS NATIONAL HAPPINESS: WHY HAPPINESS MATTERS FOR AMERICA (Basic Books 2008).

Brooks, David, Op-Ed, *The Tea Party Teens*, N.Y. TIMES, Jan. 5, 2010, at A21 (www.nytimes.com/2010/01/05/opinion/05brooks.html).

—— Op-Ed, *The Democrats Rejoice*, N.Y. TIMES, Mar. 23, 2010, at A29 (www.nytimes.com/2010/03/23/opinion/23brooks1.html).

Brown, Alex, *Steinem Keeps up the Fight*, S.F. EXAMINER, Dec. 19, 2001, at A1.

Buckingham, Marcus, FIND YOUR STRONGEST LIFE: WHAT THE HAPPIEST AND MOST SUCCESSFUL WOMEN DO DIFFERENTLY (Thomas Nelson 2009).

Bumiller, Elisabeth, *Aircraft Carrier Captain Is Removed Over His Role in Coarse Videos*, N.Y. TIMES, Jan. 5, 2011, at A11 (www.nytimes.com/2011/01/05/us/05military.html).

Buss, David & Schmitt, David, *Evolutionary psychology and feminism*, 64 SEX ROLES 768-787 (2011) (www.bradley.edu/dotAsset/196924.pdf).

Butterfield, Fox, *Women Find a New Arena for Equality: Prison*, N.Y. TIMES, Dec. 29, 2003, at A9.

Buzek, Jerzy & Reding, Viviane, Op-Ed, *Women in the Boardroom*, INT'L HERALD TRIB., Feb. 28, 2011 (www.nytimes.com/2011/03/01/opinion/01iht-edbuzek01.html).

Cahill, Larry, *Why sex matters for neuroscience*, NATURE REVIEWS NEUROSCIENCE, doi:10.1038/nrn1909, May 10, 2006.

California Department of Health Services / Tobacco Control Section, *California Tobacco Control Update* (2006) (www.cdph.ca.gov/programs/tobacco/Documents/CTCPUpdate2006.pdf).

Campaign for Tobacco-Free Kids, *California's Statewide Tobacco-Prevention Program Provides Enormous Benefits to the State* (www.tobaccofreekids.org/research/factsheets/pdf/0200.pdf).

Carey, Benedict, *Hormone Dose May Increase People's Trust in Strangers*, N.Y. Times, June 2, 2005, at A12.

—— *In a Novel Theory of Mental Disorders, Parents' Genes Are in Competition*, N.Y. Times, Nov. 11, 2008, at D4 (www.nytimes.com/2008/11/11/health/research/11brain.html).

Carvajal, Doreen, *The Female Factor: The Changing Face of Medical Care*, Int'l Herald Trib., Mar. 8, 2011 (www.nytimes.com/2011/03/08/world/europe/08iht-ffdocs08.html).

Ceci, Stephen et al., *Understanding current causes of women's underrepresentation in science*, Proceedings National Academy of Sciences USA, published online before print Feb. 7, 2011 (www.pnas.org/content/early/2011/02/02/1014871108.full.pdf).

Center for American Women and Politics, *History of Women Governors* (www.cawp.rutgers.edu/fast_facts/levels_of_office/documents/govhistory.pdf)

—— *Statewide Elective Executive Women* (www.cawp.rutgers.edu/fast_facts/levels_of_office/documents/stwidehist.pdf).

—— *Women in State Legislatures* (www.cawp.rutgers.edu/fast_facts/levels_of_office/documents/stleg.pdf).

—— *Women in the U.S. Congress* (www.cawp.rutgers.edu/fast_facts/levels_of_office/documents/cong.pdf).

—— *Women State Legislators: Leadership Positions and Committee Chairs* (www.cawp.rutgers.edu/fast_facts/levels_of_office/documents/leglead.pdf)
.

Chesler, Phyllis, Woman's Inhumanity to Woman (Thunder's Mouth/Nation Books 2002).

Chiang, Harriet, *Women speak up – big names go down: Female whistle-blowers play by "outsider" rules*, S.F. Chronicle, Jun. 17, 2002, at A1.

—— *Women Still Underrepresented on Top Rungs of Legal Profession*, S.F. Chronicle, Aug. 5, 2001, at W5.

Choo, Kristin, *Women and the Law: The Right Equation: Despite increasing numbers of female lawyers, gender equality may not be guaranteed in the future*, ABA JOURNAL, Aug. 2001, at 58.

Clark, Heather, *Study: Women underrate bosses' opinion of them*, Associated Press, SEATTLE
TIMES, Aug. 10, 2009 (seattletimes.nwsource.com/html/nationworld/20096 34354_apuswomenatwork.html).

Clark, Nicola, *The Female Factor: Getting Women into Boardrooms, by Law*, INT'L HERALD TRIB., Jan. 18, 2010
(www.nytimes.com/2010/01/28/world/europe/28iht-quota.html).

Cohen, Noam, *Define Gender Gap? Look Up Wikipedia's Contributor List*, N.Y. TIMES, Jan. 31, 2011, at A1
(www.nytimes.com/2011/01/31/business/media/31link.html).

Cohen, Patricia, *Rethinking Gender Bias in Theater*, N.Y. TIMES, Jun. 24, 2009, at C1 (www.nytimes.com/2009/06/24/theater/24play.html).

Collins, Gail, Op-Ed, *McCain's Baked Alaska*, N.Y. TIMES, Aug. 30, 2008, at A19 (www.nytimes.com/2008/08/30/opinion/30collins-.html).

—— Op-Ed, *My Favorite August*, N.Y. TIMES, Aug. 14, 2010, at A19 (www.nytimes.com/2010/08/14/opinion/14collins.html).

Conlin, Michelle, *The New Gender Gap: From kindergarten to grad school, boys are becoming the second sex*, BUSINESS WEEK, May 26, 2003, at 75.

Constable, Pamela, *Women in Iraq Decry Decision To Curb Rights; Council Backs Islamic Law on Families*, WASHINGTON POST, Jan. 16, 2004, at A12.

Corcoran, Katherine, *See Jane Not Run*, SAN FRANCISCO MAGAZINE, Jan. 2008, at 120.

Cornell, Drucilla, AT THE HEART OF FREEDOM (Princeton Univ. Press 1998).

—— THE IMAGINARY DOMAIN: ABORTION, PORNOGRAPHY AND SEXUAL HARRASSMENT (Routledge 1995).

Costa, Paul et al., *Gender Differences in Personality Traits Across Cultures: Robust and Surprising Findings*, 81 JOURNAL OF PERSONALITY AND SOCIAL PSYCHOLOGY 322 (2001).

Costello-Dougherty, Malaika, *We're Outta Here: Why Women Are Leaving Big Firms*, CALIFORNIA LAWYER, Feb. 2007, at 20.

Council, John, *Associate in Texas Alleges Pregnancy Discrimination*, TEXAS LAWYER, Apr. 5, 2004.

Creswell, Julie, *How Suite It Isn't: A Dearth of Female Bosses*, N.Y. TIMES, Dec. 17, 2006, at § 3, at 1 (www.nytimes.com/2006/12/17/business/yourmoney/17csuite.html).

Croll, E. J., *Amartya Sen's 100 Million Missing Women*, 29 OXFORD DEVELOPMENT STUDIES 225-44 (2001).

CULTURES OF MULTIPLE FATHERS (Stephen Beckerman & Paul Valentine eds., Univ. Press of Florida 2002).

Curphey, Shauna, *Amnesty Pushing Nations to End Gender Violence*, WOMEN'S ENEWS, Mar. 19, 2004 (www.womensenews.org/article.cfm?aid=1755).

Dagher, Sam, *Iraqi Women Vie for Votes and Taste of Power*, N.Y. TIMES, Jan. 29, 2009, at A6 (www.nytimes.com/2009/01/29/world/middleeast/29election.html).

Dalton, Madeline et al., *Effect of viewing smoking in movies on adolescent smoking initiation: a cohort study*, 362 LANCET 281-85 (2003).

Daly, Martin & Wilson, Margo, HOMICIDE (Aldine de Gruyter 1988).

Darwin, Charles, THE DESCENT OF MAN AND SELECTION IN RELATION TO SEX (1871).

—— THE ORIGIN OF SPECIES (1859).

Dawkins, Richard, THE SELFISH GENE (Oxford Univ. Press 1976, 2nd Ed. 1990).

Deaner, Robert, *Males Run Relatively Fast in U.S. Road Races: Further Evidence of a Sex Difference in Competitiveness*, 2006 EVOLUTIONARY PSYCHOLOGY 303 (www.gvsu.edu/cms3/assets/6D2549F6-ED41-142A-2D7251DEDEE796B4/deanerfiles/Deaner2006MoreMalesRunRelativelyFastinU.S.RoadRacesFurtherEvidenceofaSexDifferenceinCompetitiveness.pdf).

De Dreu, Carsten et al., *Oxytocin promotes human ethnocentrism*, PROCEEDINGS NATIONAL ACADEMY OF SCIENCES USA, published online before print January 10, 2011 (www.pnas.org/content/early/2011/01/06/1015316108.full.pdf+html).

—— *The Neuropeptide Oxytocin Regulates Parochial Altruism in Intergroup Conflict Among Humans*, 328 SCIENCE 1408 (June 11, 2010) (www.sciencemag.org/content/328/5984/1408.full.pdf).

Defense Task Force on Sexual Assault in the Military Services, U.S. Dep't of Defense, Dec. 2009 (www.ncdsv.org/images/SAPR_DTFSAMS_Report_Dec_2009.pdf).

Denvir, John, DEMOCRACY'S CONSTITUTION: CLAIMING THE PRIVILEGES OF AMERICAN CITIZENSHIP (Univ. of Ill. Press 2001).

Desvaux, Georges et al., *Women Matter: Gender diversity, a corporate performance driver*, McKinsey & Company, Paris 2007 (www.mckinsey.com/locations/paris/home/womenmatter/pdfs/Women_matter_oct2007_english.pdf).

Deveny, Kathleen, *Girls Gone Bad?*, NEWSWEEK, Feb. 12, 2007, at 41.

Dillon, Sam, *Harvard Chief Defends His Talk on Women*, N.Y. TIMES, Jan. 18, 2005, at A16.

Dillon, Sam & Rimer, Sara, *President of Harvard Tells Women's Panel He's Sorry*, N.Y. TIMES, Jan. 21, 2005, at A19.

Donnelly, Pat, *Feminist a la francaise: Vive la difference! Agacinski's concept of parity reaches far beyond politics*, THE GAZETTE (Montreal), Apr. 5, 2003, at A8.

Dowd, Maureen, Op-Ed, *Barbie Loves Math*, N.Y. TIMES, Feb. 6, 2002, at A21.

Dowden, Richard, *Death by Stoning*, N.Y. TIMES MAGAZINE, Jan. 27, 2002, at 28.

Duenwald, Mary, *For a Good Time, Well, Don't Call Dad*, N.Y. TIMES, Dec. 2, 2003, at F1.

—— *Who Would Abduct a Child? Previous Cases Offer Clues*, N.Y. TIMES, Aug. 27, 2002, at F1.

Duff-Brown, Beth, *Nobel Prize Winner Yunus Revered by Poor*, Associated Press, S.F. CHRONICLE, Oct. 14, 2006.

Duflo, Esther, *Women's Empowerment and Economic Development*, J. ECONOMIC LITERATURE, forthcoming (*also known as* NBER Working Paper No. 17702, 2011; CEPR Discussion Paper 8734, 2011) (http://econ-www.mit.edu/files/7417).

Dugger, Celia, *African Studies Give Women Hope in H.I.V. Fight*, N.Y. TIMES, Jul. 20, 2010, at A1 (www.nytimes.com/2010/07/20/world/africa/20safrica.html).

—— *In Africa, Free Schools Feed a Different Hunger*, N.Y. TIMES, Oct. 24, 2004, § 1, at 1.

Eagleton Institute of Politics, *Political Generation Next: Young, Ambitious, and a Lot Like Their Elders?*, 2003.

Editorial, *A Promising Preventive*, N.Y. TIMES, Jul. 21, 2010, at A26 (www.nytimes.com/2010/07/21/opinion/21wed2.html).

Editorial, *How Bush Treats Women*, BOSTON GLOBE, March 17, 2004, at A14.

Editorial, *The Hypocrisy of Farm Subsidies*, N.Y. TIMES, Dec. 1, 2002, § 4, at 8.

Editorial, *Window of Opportunity*, S.F. CHRONICLE, Dec. 19, 2001, at A26.

Ember, C., *Myths about hunter-gatherers*, 4 ETHNOLOGY 439-48 (1978).

Engel, Susan & Sandstrom, Marlene, Op-Ed, *There's Only One Way to Stop a Bully*, N.Y. TIMES, Jul. 23, 2010, at A23 (www.nytimes.com/2010/07/23/opinion/23engel.html).

Equality in Job Loss: Women Are Increasingly Vulnerable to Layoffs During Recessions, Majority Staff Report of the Joint Congressional Economic Committee, July, 22, 2008 (http://jec.senate.gov/public/?a=Files.Serve&File_id=80a7a0cd-6125-495d -bca5-09af2c0393f9).

Etcoff, Nancy, SURVIVAL OF THE PRETTIEST: THE SCIENCE OF BEAUTY (Doubleday 1999).

Etcoff, Nancy et al., *Cosmetics as a Feature of the Extended Human Phenotype: Modulation of the Perception of Biologically Important Facial Signals*, PLoS ONE 6(10): e25656. doi:10.1371 (www.plosone.org/article/info:doi%2F10.1371%2Fjournal.pone.0025656).

Evans, Gail, SHE WINS, YOU WIN: A GUIDEBOOK FOR MAKING WOMEN MORE POWERFUL (Gotham Books 2003).

Fagan, Kevin, *A new battle of the sexes; Men and women view the war and its coverage with fundamental differences*, S.F. CHRONICLE, Mar. 28, 2003, at W9.

Faludi, Susan, BACKLASH: THE UNDECLARED WAR AGAINST AMERICAN WOMEN (Crown 1991).

Fang, Bay, *The Talibanization of Iraq*, MS. MAGAZINE (Spring 2007) (www.msmagazine.com/spring2007/taliban.asp).

Farah, May, *Arab Women Savor Patches of Political Progress*, WOMEN'S ENEWS, Jul. 14, 2004 (womensenews.org/story/the-world/040714/arab-women-savor-patches-pol itical-progress).

Fathi, Nazila, *Iraqi Career Women Ponder a Future Under Shiite Rule*, N.Y. TIMES, May 25, 2003, § 1, at 19.

Ferrary, Michel, *Why women managers shine in a downturn*, FINANCIAL TIMES, Mar. 2, 2009 (www.generation-europe.eu/community/img/posts/2010/04/potw_2009-03-02.pdf).

Fisher, Helen E., THE FIRST SEX: THE NATURAL TALENTS OF WOMEN AND HOW THEY ARE CHANGING THE WORLD (Ballantine Books 2000).

Flanagan, Caitlin, *Op-Ed, Hysteria and the Teenage Girl*, N.Y. TIMES, Jan. 29, 2012, at SR4 (www.nytimes.com/2012/01/29/opinion/sunday/adolescent-girl-hysteria.html).

Ford, Dave, *Battling the bullies: S.F. filmmaker turns her lens on schoolyard tyrants in an effort to change a painful culture*, S.F. CHRONICLE, Apr. 2, 2004, at F1.

Freeland, Chrystia, *Way of the World: Equal Rights Make Sense for U.S. Economy*, INT'L HERALD TRIB., May 18, 2012 (www.nytimes.com/2012/05/18/us/18iht-letter18.html?smid=pl-share).

Freud, Sigmund & Breuer, Josef, STUDIES IN HYSTERIA (trans. Luckhurst, Nicola & Bowlby, Rachel, Penguin Classics 2004).

Fukuyama, Francis, *Women and the Evolution of World Politics*, FOREIGN AFFAIRS, Sept./Oct. 1998, at 24 (www.metu.edu.tr/~utuba/Fukuyama.pdf).

Gale, Patrick, ARMISTEAD MAUPIN (Absolute Press 1999).

Galinsky, Ellen et al., *2008 National Study of the Changing Workforce*, Families and Work Institute (familiesandwork.org/site/research/reports/Times_Are_Changing.pdf).

Gall, Carlotta, *Afghan Motherhood in a Fight for Survival*, N.Y. TIMES, May 25, 2003, § 1, at 3.

Ganahal, Jane, *Finding their voices; Training program helps women shape political dreams*, S.F. CHRONICLE, Feb. 23, 2003, at E1.

Gangestad, Steven W. et al., *Changes in women's sexual interests and their partners' mate retention tactics across the menstrual cycle: evidence for shifting conflicts of interest*, 269 PROCEEDINGS OF THE ROYAL SOCIETY B: BIOLOGICAL SCIENCES, 975-82 (May 7, 2002).

Garbarino, James, LOST BOYS: WHY OUR SONS TURN VIOLENT AND HOW WE CAN SAVE THEM (Free Press 1999).

General Accounting Office, *Women's Earnings: Work Patterns Partially Explain Difference between Men's and Women's Earnings*, Oct. 2003.

Gentleman, Amelia, *Theresa May scraps legal requirement to reduce inequality*, Guardian, Nov. 17, 2010 (www.guardian.co.uk/society/2010/nov/17/theresa-may-scraps-legal-requirement-inequality).

Gettleman, Jeffrey, *Fighting Congo's Ills With Education and an Army of Women*, N.Y. Times, Feb. 7, 2011, at A6 (www.nytimes.com/2011/02/07/world/africa/07congo.html).

—— *Rapes Total In Millions In Congo, Study Finds*, N.Y. Times, May 12, 2011, at A4 (www.nytimes.com/2011/05/12/world/africa/12congo.html).

—— *Rwanda Stirs Deadly Brew of Troubles in Congo*, N.Y. Times, Dec. 4, 2008, at A6 (www.nytimes.com/2008/12/04/world/africa/04congo.html).

Gettler, Lee et al., *Longitudinal evidence that fatherhood decreases testosterone in human males*, Proceedings National Academy of Sciences USA, published online before print Sept. 12, 2011 (www.pnas.org/content/early/2011/09/02/1105403108.full.pdf+html).

Gibbs, Nancy, *Sexual Assaults on Female Soldiers: Don't Ask, Don't Tell*, Time Magazine, Mar. 8, 2010 (www.time.com/time/magazine/article/0,9171,1968110,00.html).

Gilligan, Carol, In a Different Voice: Psychological Theory and the Women's Movement (Harvard Univ. Press 1982).

Gilman, Charlotte Perkins, Herland (Pantheon Books 1979) (1915).

Giridharadas, Anand, *Currents: Questioning Alpha Leadership*, Int'l Herald Trib., Jun. 30, 2012 (www.nytimes.com/2012/06/30/us/30iht-letter30.html?smid=pl-share).

Gladwell, Malcolm, The Tipping Point: How Little Things Can Make a Big Difference (Little, Brown & Co. 2000).

Goldstein, Joshua S., War and Gender: How Gender Shapes the War System and Vice Versa (Cambridge Univ. Press 2001).

Goode, Erica, *Human Nature: Born Or Made?*, N.Y. Times, Mar. 14, 2000, at F1.

Gootman, Elissa, *Bloomberg Discrimination-Suit Ruling Renews Work-Life Debate*, N.Y. Times, Aug. 19, 2011, at A18 (www.nytimes.com/2011/08/19/nyregion/bloomberg-discrimination-suit-ruling-renews-work-life-debate.html).

Gould, Stephen Jay & Lewontin, Richard C., *The Spandrels of San Marco and the Panglossian Paradigm: a critique of the adaptationist program*, 205 PROCEEDINGS OF THE ROYAL SOCIETY B: BIOLOGICAL SCIENCES 581-98 (1979).

Grainger, Heidi & Holt, Heather, *Results of the Second Flexible Working Employee Survey*, Office for National Statistics, Labour Market Trends, July 2005 (www.ons.gov.uk/ons/rel/lms/labour-market-trends--discontinued-/volume-113--no--7/results-of-the-second-flexible-working-employee-survey.pdf).

Greenhouse, Linda, *Supreme Court to Review Using Execution in Juvenile Cases*, N.Y. TIMES, Jan. 27, 2004, at A1.

Growthink Research, VENTURE FUNDING FOR WOMEN ENTREPRENEURS (2004).

Guinier, Lani et al., *Becoming Gentlemen: Women's Experiences at One Ivy League Law School*, 143 UNIV. PENN. LAW REV. 1 (1994).

Haidt, Jonathan, THE RIGHTEOUS MIND: WHY GOOD PEOPLE ARE DIVIDED BY POLITICS AND RELIGION (Pantheon 2012).

Hall, Carl T., *Study finds genetic link to violence*, S.F. CHRONICLE, Aug. 2, 2002, at A2.

Hamermesh, Daniel, BEAUTY PAYS: WHY ATTRACTIVE PEOPLE ARE MORE SUCCESSFUL (Princeton Univ. Press 2011).

Harris, Judith, THE NURTURE ASSUMPTION: WHY CHILDREN TURN OUT THE WAY THEY DO (Free Press 1998).

Hartmann, Heidi et al., *Memo to John Roberts: The Gender Wage Gap is Real*, Institute for Women's Policy Research Fact Sheet #C362, Sept. 2005.

Hass, Nancy, *Gloria Steinem Still Wants More*, NEWSWEEK, Aug. 15, 2011, at 54.

Haugen, Gary, Op-Ed, *State's Blind Eye on Sexual Slavery*, WASHINGTON POST, Jun. 15, 2002, at A23.

Haughney, Christine, *Women, Uneasy, Still Lag as Cyclists in New York City*, N.Y. TIMES, Jul. 4, 2011, at A13 (www.nytimes.com/2011/07/04/nyregion/number-of-female-cyclists-lags-in-new-york-with-safety-as-a-concern.html).

Hausmann, Ricardo et al, *The Global Gender Gap Report 2011*, World Economic Forum (Geneva, Swit.) (www3.weforum.org/docs/WEF_GenderGap_Report_2011.pdf).

Havlicek, Jan et al., *Women's preference for dominant male odour: effects of menstrual cycle and relationship status*, Biology Letters, doi:10.1098/rsbl.2005.0332 (www.natur.cuni.cz/~flegr/pdf/domin.pdf).

Hayek, F.A., The Road to Serfdom: Text and Documents – The Definitive Edition (The Collected Works of F. A. Hayek, Volume 2) (Univ. of Chicago Press 2007).

—— *Why I Am Not a Conservative, in* The Constitution of Liberty (Univ. of Chicago Press 1960).

Hegewisch, Ariane et al., *Briefing Paper: Separate and Not Equal? Gender Segregation in the Labor Market and the Gender Wage Gap* (Wash., D.C., Inst. for Women's Policy Research, Sept. 2010).

Hegewisch, Ariane & Gornick, Janet, *Statutory Routes to Workplace Flexibility in Cross-National Perspective* (Wash., D.C., Inst. for Women's Policy Research, May 2008) (www.worklifelaw.org/pubs/Statutory%20Routes%20to%20WkFlex.pdf).

Hegewisch, Ariane & Williams, Claudia, *The Gender Wage Gap: 2010* (Wash., D.C., Inst. for Women's Policy Research, Sept. 2011).

Helgesen, Sally, The Female Advantage: Women's Ways of Leadership (Currency/Doubleday 1995).

Hendricks, Tyche, *U.S. court rules rape is grounds for asylum; Guatemalan granted a new hearing before immigration board*, S.F. Chronicle, Jun. 16, 2004, at A1.

Hennessey John, Hockfield, Susan & Tilghman, Shirley, Op-Ed, Women and Science: the Real Issue, Boston Globe, Feb. 12, 2005, at A13.

Heredia, Christopher, *UCSF study ignites drive to stop smoking in kids' movies*, S.F. Chronicle, Apr. 2, 2004, at F1.

Hesselbein, Frances, Hesselbein on Leadership (Jossey-Bass 2002).

Hewlett, Sylvia Ann, Creating a Life: Professional Women and the Quest for Children (Talk Miramax Books 2002).

—— Off-ramps and On-ramps: Keeping Talented Women on the Road to Success (Harvard Business School Press 2007).

Hill, Anita F., Op-Ed, *Insider Women With Outsider Values*, N.Y. Times, Jun. 6, 2002, at A31.

Hill, Catherine, et al., *Why So Few? Women in Science, Technology, Engineering, and Mathematics*, Amer. Ass'n Univ. Women, Feb. 2010 (www.aauw.org/learn/research/whysofew.cfm).

HIP-HOP: BEYOND BEATS & RHYMES (Media Education Foundation 2006).

Ho, R., *Gender gap narrows for credit-seekers*, WALL STREET JOURNAL, Apr. 9, 1997, at B2.

Hockstader, Lee, *Palestinians Hail a Heroine; Israelis See Rising Threat*, WASHINGTON POST, Jan. 31, 2002, at A20.

Hoffman, Saul, *By the Numbers: The Public Costs of Teen Childbearing*, National Campaign to Prevent Teen Pregnancy (2006) (www.thenationalcampaign.org/costs/pdf/report/BTN_National_Report.pdf).

Horton-Flaherty, Kristina, *Women lawyers in balancing act*, CALIFORNIA BAR JOURNAL, Feb. 2002, at 1.

Hrdy, Sarah B., MOTHER NATURE: MATERNAL INSTINCTS AND HOW THEY SHAPE THE HUMAN SPECIES (Ballantine Books 1999).

—— THE WOMAN THAT NEVER EVOLVED (Harvard Univ. Press 1981, 1999 Ed.).

Hu, Winnie, *Gossip Girls and Boys Stop to Empathize*, N.Y. TIMES, Apr. 5, 2009, at A1 (www.nytimes.com/2009/04/05/education/05empathy.html).

Hua, Vanessa, *Cracks widen in glass ceiling: Women top execs increase numbers*, S.F. CHRONICLE, Nov. 19, 2002, at B1.

Hudson, Valerie & den Boer, Andrea, BARE BRANCHES: THE SECURITY IMPLICATIONS OF ASIA'S SURPLUS MALE POPULATION (MIT Press 2005).

International Institute for Democracy and Electoral Assistance, *Women in Parliaments: Beyond Numbers* (2nd Ed. 2005) (www.idea.int/publications/wip2).

Inter-Parliamentary Union, *Women in National Parliaments* (www.ipu.org/wmn-e/classif.htm).

Jacoby, Susan, THE AGE OF AMERICAN UNREASON (Pantheon 2008).

James, Andrea & Tartakoff, Joseph, *The Insider: Starbucks picks up a little free publicity from bungled quote*, SEATTLE POST INTELLIGENCER, Oct. 8, 2008 (www.seattlepi.com/business/382971_theinsider13.html).

Janofsky, Michael, *Air Force Begins an Inquiry of Ex-Cadets' Rape Charges*, N.Y. TIMES, Feb. 20, 2003, at A18.

—— *General Asks Air Force to Build Trust at Academy*, N.Y. TIMES, Feb. 21, 2003, at A18.

Janofsky, Michael, with Schemo, Diana Jean, *Women Recount Life as Cadets: Forced Sex, Fear and Silent Rage*, N.Y. TIMES, Mar. 14, 2003, § 1, at 1.

Jargon, Julie, *The War Within*, WESTWORD, Jan. 30, 2003.

Jefferson, Thomas, letter to William Stephens Smith, Paris, Nov. 13, 1787 (wiki.monticello.org/mediawiki/index.php/The_tree_of_liberty...(Quotation)).

Jha, Prabhat et al., *Trends in selective abortions of girls in India: analysis of nationally representative birth histories from 1990 to 2005 and census data from 1991 to 2011*, THE LANCET, Early Online Publication, May 24, 2011 (www.thelancet.com/journals/lancet/article/PIIS0140-6736(11)60649-1/fulltext).

Jones, Maggie, *The Weaker Sex*, N.Y. TIMES MAGAZINE, Mar. 16, 2003, at 56.

Juska, Jane, A ROUND-HEELED WOMAN: MY LATE-LIFE ADVENTURES IN SEX AND ROMANCE (Villard Books 2003).

Kane, Jonathan & Mertz, Janet, *Debunking Myths about Gender and Mathematics Performance*, 59 NOTICES OF THE AMERICAN MATHEMATICAL SOCIETY 10 (2012) (www.ams.org/notices/201201/rtx120100010p.pdf).

Kauffman Foundation, *Gatekeepers of Venture Growth: The Role and Participation of Women in the Venture Capital Industry*, 2004 (www.kauffman.org/pages/416.cfm).

Kimmel, Michael S., THE GENDERED SOCIETY (Oxford Univ. Press 2000).

Kirp, David L., *Life Way After Head Start*, N.Y. TIMES, Nov. 21, 2004, at § 6, at 32.

Klaus, Peggy, Op-Ed, *Preoccupations: A Sisterhood of Workplace Infighting*, N.Y. TIMES, Jan. 11, 2009, at BU2 (www.nytimes.com/2009/01/11/jobs/11pre.html).

Knight, Heather, *Celebrating the Clitoris*, S.F. CHRONICLE, Mar. 9, 2003, at E1.

Kolata, Gina, *Men, Women and Speed. 2 Words: Got Testosterone?*, N.Y. TIMES, Aug. 22, 2008, at D1 (www.nytimes.com/2008/08/22/sports/olympics/22women.html).

Komisaruk, Barry et al., THE SCIENCE OF ORGASM (Johns Hopkins Univ. Press 2006).

Koopman, John, *A few good women Marines make history at forward bases*, S.F. CHRONICLE, Mar. 16, 2003, at A8.

Koppel, Naomi, *UNICEF: Millions of girls uneducated*, S.F. CHRONICLE, Dec. 12, 2003 at A14.

Kornbluh, Karen, *The Parent Trap*, THE ATLANTIC MONTHLY, Jan./Feb. 2003, at 111.

Kosfeld, Michael et al., *Oxytocin increases trust in humans*, 435 NATURE 673-676 (2005).

Kraft, Dina, *Israel Warriors Find Machismo Is Way of Past*, N.Y. TIMES, Oct. 19, 2006, at A1.

Kramer, Andrew, *Blasts Revive Russians' Fear of Female Bombers*, N.Y. TIMES, Mar. 30, 2010, at A8 (www.nytimes.com/2010/03/30/world/europe/30blackwidows.html).

Kramer, Vicki W. et al., *Critical Mass on Corporate Boards: Why Three or More Women Enhance Governance* (Wellesley Centers for Women 2006).

Kristof, Nicholas, interview on *It's Your World* (World Affairs Council broadcast on KQED radio, *Turning Oppression into Opportunity for Women Worldwide*, San Francisco, Ca., Oct. 19, 2009).

—— Op-Ed, *Bush vs. Women*, N.Y. TIMES, Aug. 16, 2002, at A17.

—— Op-Ed, *Girls for Sale*, N.Y. TIMES, Jan. 17, 2004, at A15.

—— Op-Ed, *How to Raise Our I.Q.*, N.Y. TIMES, Apr. 16, 2009, at A29 (www.nytimes.com/2009/04/16/opinion/16kristof.html).

—— Op-Ed, *Sentenced to Be Raped*, N.Y. TIMES, Sept. 29, 2004, at A25.

—— Op-Ed, *The Face of Modern Slavery*, N.Y. TIMES, Nov. 17, 2011, at A31 (www.nytimes.com/2011/11/17/opinion/kristof-the-face-of-modern-slavery .html).

—— Op-Ed, *The Happiest People*, N.Y. TIMES, Jan. 7, 2010, at A31 (www.nytimes.com/2010/01/07/opinion/07kristof.html).

—— Op-Ed, *Women's Rights: Why Not?*, N.Y. TIMES, Jun. 18, 2002, at A23.

Kristof, Nicholas & Wudunn, Sheryl, *The Women's Crusade*, N.Y. TIMES MAGAZINE, Aug. 24, 2009, at 28 (www.nytimes.com/2009/08/23/magazine/23Women-t.html).

Kuczynski, Alex, *The New Feminist Mystique; Variety of Brash Magazines Upset the Old Stereotypes*, N.Y. TIMES, Sept. 10, 2001, at C1.

Kulish, Nicholas, *Aided by Safety Nets, Europe Resists Stimulus Push*, N.Y. TIMES, Mar. 27, 2009, at A1 (www.nytimes.com/2009/03/27/world/europe/27germany.html).

Kuchment, Anna, *The Tangled Web of Porn in the Office*, NEWSWEEK, Nov. 29, 2008 (www.newsweek.com/2008/11/28/the-tangled-web-of-porn-in-the-office.html).

Lacayo, Richard & Ripley, Amanda, *Persons of the Year*, TIME, Dec. 22, 2002, at 30.

Lacey, Marc, *Women's Voices Rise as Rwanda Reinvents Itself*, N.Y. TIMES, Feb. 26, 2005, at A1.

LaFraniere, Sharon, *Chinese Bias for Baby Boys Creates a Gap of 32 Million*, N.Y. TIMES, Apr. 11, 2009, at A5 (www.nytimes.com/2009/04/11/world/asia/11china.html).

Lamb, Christina, *"Ministry of vice" fills Afghan women with fear*, THE TIMES (London), Jul. 23, 2006.

Landesman, Peter, *The Girls Next Door*, N.Y. TIMES MAGAZINE, Jan. 25, 2004, at 30.

—— *A Woman's Work*, N.Y. TIMES MAGAZINE, Sept. 15, 2002, at 82.

Laurence, L. & Spalter-Roth, R., *Measuring the Costs of Domestic Violence Against Women and the Cost-Effectiveness of Interventions: An Initial Assessment and Proposals for Further Research* (Wash., D.C., Inst. for Women's Policy Research, May 1996).

Lawless, Jennifer & Fox, Richard, IT TAKES A CANDIDATE: WHY WOMEN DON'T RUN FOR OFFICE (Cambridge Univ. Press 2005).

Leake, Jonathan, *Women are getting more beautiful*, THE TIMES (London), Jul. 26, 2009.

Leakey, Richard E. & Lewin, Roger, ORIGINS: THE EMERGENCE AND EVOLUTION OF OUR SPECIES AND ITS POSSIBLE FUTURE (E.P. Dutton, Inc. 1977, 1982).

Lederer, Edith, *U.S. challenges U.N. over abortion right*, Associated Press, S.F. CHRONICLE, Feb. 28, 2005, at A5.

Lehrman, Sally, *The virtues of promiscuity*, S.F. CHRONICLE, Aug. 18, 2002, at D1.

Lennon, John & Ono, Yoko, *Woman is the Nigger of the World*, SHAVED FISH (Emd/Capitol 1975).

Leonhardt, David, *Economic Scene: A Labor Market Punishing to Mothers*, N.Y. TIMES, Aug. 4, 2010, at B1 (www.nytimes.com/2010/08/04/business/economy/04leonhardt.html).

—— *Gender Pay Gap, Once Narrowing, Is Stuck in Place*, N.Y. TIMES, Dec. 24, 2006, § 1, at 1 (www.nytimes.com/2006/12/24/business/24gap.html).

Levy, Ariel, FEMALE CHAUVINIST PIGS: WOMEN AND THE RISE OF RAUNCH CULTURE (Free Press 2005).

Lévy-Bruhl, Lucien, HOW NATIVES THINK (1910, trans. Lilian A. Clare 1926, reprinted Princeton Univ. Press 1985).

Lewin, Tamar, *Bias Called Persistent Hurdle for Women in Sciences*, N.Y. TIMES, Mar. 22, 2010, at A14 (www.nytimes.com/2010/03/22/science/22women.html).

—— *Little Sympathy or Remedy For Inmates Who Are Raped*, N.Y. TIMES, Apr. 15, 2001, § 1, at 1.

Lightdale, J.R., & Prentice, D.A., *Rethinking sex differences in aggression: Aggressive behaviour in the absence of social roles*, 20 PERSONALITY AND SOCIAL PSYCHOLOGY BULLETIN 34-44 (1994).

Little, A.C. et al., *Partnership status and the temporal context of relationships influence human female preferences for sexual dimorphism in male face shape*, 269 PROCEEDINGS OF THE ROYAL SOCIETY B: BIOLOGICAL SCIENCES 1095-1100 (Jun. 7, 2002) (rspb.royalsocietypublishing.org/content/269/1496/1095.full.pdf).

Littleton, Christine, *Reconstructing Sexual Equality*, 75 CAL. LAW REV. 1279 (1987).

Locke, John, CONCERNING CIVIL GOVERNMENT, SECOND ESSAY: AN ESSAY CONCERNING THE TRUE ORIGINAL EXTENT AND END OF CIVIL GOVERNMENT (W. B. Eerdmans Pub. Co. (1978) (1690).

Lo Sasso, Anthony et al., *The $16,819 Pay Gap For Newly Trained Physicians: The Unexplained Trend Of Men Earning More Than Women*, 30 HEALTH AFFAIRS 193 (Feb. 2011).

Machacek, John, *Poll finds voters skeptical about a woman president*, Gannett News Service, Feb. 23, 2006 (citing WNBC/Marist Poll at pp. 8-9, maristpoll.marist.edu/wp-content/misc/usapolls/HC060222.pdf).

MacKinnon, Catharine, TOWARD A FEMINIST THEORY OF THE STATE (Harvard Univ. Press 1989).

Maines, Rachel, THE TECHNOLOGY OF ORGASM: "HYSTERIA," THE VIBRATOR, AND WOMEN'S SEXUAL SATISFACTION (Johns Hopkins Univ. Press 1998).

Marquis, Christopher, *U.S. Cuts Off Financing of U.N. Unit for 3rd Year*, N.Y. TIMES, Jul. 17, 2004, at A6.

Mason, Mary Ann, THE EQUALITY TRAP (Touchstone 1988).

Mathews Fiona et al., *You are what your mother eats: Evidence for maternal preconception diet influencing foetal sex in humans*, PROCEEDINGS OF THE ROYAL SOCIETY B, doi:10.1098/rspb.2008.0105 (rspb.royalsocietypublishing.org/content/275/1643/1661.full.pdf+html).

May, Elaine Tyler, Op-Ed, *Promises the Pill Could Never Keep*, N.Y. TIMES, Apr. 25, 2010, at WK13 (www.nytimes.com/2010/04/25/opinion/25may.html).

McGinn, Daniel, *Getting Back on Track*, NEWSWEEK, Sept. 25, 2006, at 62.

McKinley, James, *She Ran to Gunfire, and Ended It*, N.Y. TIMES, Nov. 7, 2009, at A1 (www.nytimes.com/2009/11/07/us/07police.html).

McKinley, Jesse, *A Tax on Nips and Tucks Angers Patients, Surgeons*, N.Y. TIMES, Nov. 30, 2009, at A14 (www.nytimes.com/2009/11/30/health/policy/30cosmetic.html).

McNeil, Donald G., Jr., *Billionaires Back Antismoking Effort*, N.Y. TIMES, Jul. 24, 2008 (www.nytimes.com/2008/07/24/health/24tobacco.html)

Meece, Mickey, *What Do Women Want? Just Ask*, N.Y. TIMES, Oct. 29, 2006, § 3, at 1.

Michaels, Jim, *Iraq's female lawmakers making strides*, USA TODAY, Oct 27, 2008, at 11A (www.usatoday.com/news/world/iraq/2008-10-26-iraqwomen_N.htm).

Michel, Lou & Herbeck, Dan, AMERICAN TERRORIST: TIMOTHY MCVEIGH AND THE OKLAHOMA CITY BOMBING (Harper 2001).

Military Personnel: DOD's and the Coast Guard's Sexual Assault Prevention and Response Programs Face Implementation and Oversight Challenges, Government Accountability Office, GAO-08-924 Aug. 29, 2008 (www.gao.gov/products/GAO-08-924).

Miller, Claire, *Out of the Loop in Silicon Valley*, N.Y. TIMES, Apr. 18, 2010, at BU1 (www.nytimes.com/2010/04/18/technology/18women.html).

Miller, Geoffrey, THE MATING MIND: HOW SEXUAL CHOICE SHAPED THE EVOLUTION OF HUMAN NATURE (Doubleday 2000).

Miller, Kevin, *Child Care Support for Student Parents in Community College Is Crucial for Success, but Supply and Funding Are Inadequate*, Institute for Women's Policy Research Fact Sheet #C375, June 2010 (www.iwpr. org/publications/pubs/child-care-support-for-student-parents-in-community -college-is-crucial-for-success-but-supply-and-funding-are- inadequate/at_download/file).

Miller, Saul & Maner, Jon, *Evolution and relationship maintenance: Fertility cues lead committed men to devalue relationship alternatives*, 46 JOURNAL OF EXPERIMENTAL SOCIAL PSYCHOLOGY 1081 (2010) (www.uky.edu/~slmi227/evolution_and_relationship_maintenance.pdf).

Miller-Medzon, Karyn, *Finding the formula for love – Love's true chemistry is heaven scent*, BOSTON HERALD, February 13, 2000, Arts & Leisure Sec., at 46.

Moffeit, Miles & Herdy, Amy, *Betrayal in the Ranks*, DENVER POST, Nov. 16-18, 2003, at A1 (http://extras.denverpost.com/justice/tdp_betrayal.pdf).

Momigliano, Anna, *Italy's end to employment discrimination has women crying foul*, CHRISTIAN SCIENCE MONITOR, Sept. 1, 2009.

Moncrief, Gary et al., WHO RUNS FOR THE LEGISLATURE? (Prentice-Hall 2001).

Morell, V., *A new look at monogamy*, 281 SCIENCE 1982-83 (1998).

Morris, Desmond, INTIMATE BEHAVIOR: A ZOOLOGIST'S CLASSIC STUDY OF HUMAN INTIMACY (Random House 1971).

Moss, Michael, *Pentagon Faces New Questions on Old Problem*, N.Y. TIMES, Mar. 2, 2003, § 1, at 26.

Mullan, Peter, interview on *Fresh Air* (NPR Radio broadcast, Aug. 12, 2003).

Murdock, G.P., ETHNOGRAPHIC ATLAS (Univ. of Pittsburgh Press 1967).

Murphy, Clare, *Le Pen and his feminine side*, BBC News Online, May 28, 2002 (news.bbc.co.uk/1/hi/world/europe/2011370.stm).

Murray, Charles, Op-Ed, *Sex Ed at Harvard*, N.Y. TIMES, Jan. 23, 2005, at § 4, at 17.

Myers, Dee Dee, WHY WOMEN SHOULD RULE THE WORLD (Harper 2008).

Myers, Steven L., *Another Peril in War Zones: Sexual Abuse by Fellow G.I.'s*, N.Y. TIMES, Dec. 28, 2009, at A1 (www.nytimes.com/2009/12/28/us/28women.html).

—— *From Dismal Chechnya, Women Turn to Bombs*, N.Y. TIMES, Sept. 10, 2004, at A1.

Nance-Nash, Sheryl, *Fewer Employers Offering Flexible Schedules*, WOMEN'S ENEWS, Dec. 16, 2004 (www.womensenews.org/article.cfm?aid=2109).

National Academy of Sciences, *Beyond Bias and Barriers: Fulfilling the Potential of Women in Academic Science and Engineering*, Sept. 2006 (newton.nap.edu/execsumm_pdf/11741).

National Center for Women & Policing, *Hiring & Retaining More Women: The Advantages to Law Enforcement Agencies* (2003) (www.womenandpolicing.org/pdf/NewAdvantagesReport.pdf).

National Conference of State Legislatures, *Supermajority Vote Requirements* (2012) (www.ncsl.org/programs/legismgt/elect/SupermajVote.htm).

Nebesar, Darren Anne, Note, *Gender-Based Violence as a Weapon of War*, 4 U.C. DAVIS J. INT'L L. & POL'Y 147 (1998).

Noer, Michael, *Don't Marry Career Women*, FORBES MAGAZINE, Aug. 22, 2006 (www.forbes.com/2006/08/23/Marriage-Careers-Divorce_cx_mn_land.html).

Nusbaum, Marci Alboher, *Executive Life; Lawyers Push to Keep the Office at Bay*, N.Y. TIMES, Sept. 7, 2003, § 1, at 13.

O'Connor, Sandra Day, *Portia's Progress*, 66 N.Y.U. L. REV. 1546 (1991).

Oochy, woochy, coochy, coo, ECONOMIST, May 13, 2006, at 92.

Omang, Joanne, *U.S. Isolated on International Women's Health*, WOMEN'S ENEWS, Mar. 14, 2004 (oldsite.womensenews.org/article.cfm/dyn/aid/1749/context/archive).

Oster, Emily, *Hepatitis B and the Case of the Missing Women*, 113 JOURNAL OF POLITICAL ECONOMY 1163-216 (2005).

Oster, Emily & Thornton, Rebecca, *Menstruation and Education in Nepal*, Nat. Bur. of Economics Research Working Paper No. 14853, Apr. 2009 (www.nber.org/papers/w14853).

Parker, Ashley, *Lawsuit Says Military Is Rife With Sexual Abuse*, N.Y. TIMES, Feb. 15, 2011, at A18 (www.nytimes.com/2011/02/16/us/16military.html).

Parker-Pope, Tara, *Well: Love, Sex and the Changing Landscape of Infidelity*, N.Y. TIMES, Oct. 28, 2008, at D1 (www.nytimes.com/2008/10/28/health/28well.html).

Patten, Wendy L. & Ward, J. Andrew, *Recent Developments: Empowering Women to Stop Aids in Cote D'ivoire and Uganda*, 6 HARV. HUM. RTS. J. 210 (1993).

Paul, Pamela, *The Playground Gets Even Tougher*, N.Y. TIMES, Oct. 10, 2010 at ST12 (www.nytimes.com/2010/10/10/fashion/10Cultural.html).

Pechmann, Cornelia et al., *What to Convey in Antismoking Advertisements for Adolescents: The Use of Protection Motivation Theory to Identify Effective Message Themes*, 67 J. MARKETING 1-18 (Apr. 2003) (web.gsm.uci.edu/antismokingads/articles/trdrp3jm.pdf).

Penton-Voak, Ian S. et al., *Female Condition Influences Preferences for Sexual Dimorphism in Faces of Male Humans*, 117 J. COMPARATIVE PSYCHOLOGY 264-71 (2003) (www.alittlelab.stir.ac.uk/pubs/pentonvoak_03_whr_mascprefs_jcp.pdf).

Peresie, Jennifer, Note, *Female Judges Matter: Gender and Collegial Decisionmaking in the Federal Appellate Courts*, 114 YALE LAW J. 1759 (2005) (www.yalelawjournal.org/images/pdfs/211.pdf).

Pinker, Steven, THE BLANK SLATE: THE MODERN DENIAL OF HUMAN NATURE (Viking Press 2002).

Playing Away: Women are most attracted by infidelity when most susceptible to impregnation, ECONOMIST, May 4, 2002 (www.economist.com/node/1109532).

Polansky, Jonathan R. & Glantz, Stanton A., *First-Run Smoking Presentations in U.S. Movies 1999-2003*, Center for Tobacco Control Research and Education (March 9, 2004) (http://escholarship.org/uc/item/5hj06178).

Polgreen, Lydia, *Militias in Congo Tied to Government and Rwanda*, N.Y. TIMES, Dec. 13, 2008, at A5 (www.nytimes.com/2008/12/13/world/africa/13congo.html).

Polk, Michael F., Note, *Women Persecuted Under Islamic Law: The Zina Ordinance in Pakistan as a Basis for Asylum Claims in the United States*, 12 GEO. IMMIGR. L.J. 379 (1998).

Prasad, Raekha & Ramesh, Randeep, *India's missing girls*, GUARDIAN, Feb. 28, 2007, at 4 (www.guardian.co.uk/world/2007/feb/28/india.raekhaprasad).

Rampell, Catherine, *Still Few Women in Management, Report Says*, N.Y. TIMES, Sept. 28, 2010, at B1 (www.nytimes.com/2010/09/28/business/28gender.html).

Randall, Alice, Op-Ed, *Black Women and Fat*, N.Y. TIMES, May 6, 2012, at SR5 (www.nytimes.com/2012/05/06/opinion/sunday/why-black-women-are-fat. html?smid=pl-share).

Rawls, John, A THEORY OF JUSTICE (Harvard Univ. Press 1971).

Reich, Charles A., THE GREENING OF AMERICA (Random House 1970).

—— OPPOSING THE SYSTEM (Crown Publishers 1995).

Reid, T. R., *Academy Probes Assaults; Female Air Force Cadets Allegedly Punished for Reporting Rapes*, Washington Post, Feb. 21, 2003, at A4.

Report of the Fourth Annual National Survey on Retention and Promotion of Women in Law Firms, Nat'l Ass'n of Women Lawyers, Oct. 2009.

Resnik, Judith, *Categorical Federalism: Jurisdiction, Gender, and the Globe*, 111 YALE L.J. 619 (2001).

Revkin, Andrew, *Gore Alliance Starts Ad Campaign on Global Warming*, N.Y. TIMES, Apr. 1, 2008, at C8. (www.nytimes.com/2008/04/01/business/media/01green.html).

Rhode, Deborah L., *Feminist Critical Theories*, 42 STANFORD LAW REV. 617 (1990).

Rich, Adrienne, *Disloyal to the Civilization*, *in* ON LIES, SECRETS AND SILENCE 279-310 (Norton 1979).

Rich, Motoko, *It's the Economy, Honey*, N.Y. TIMES, Feb. 12, 2012, at BU1 (www.nytimes.com/2012/02/12/business/economics-of-family-life-as-taug ht-by-a-power-couple.html).

Ridge, Mian. *The Female Factor: Women Spreading Political Wings With Help of India's Quota System*, INT'L HERALD TRIB., April 28, 2010 (www.nytimes.com/2010/04/28/world/asia/28iht-quotas.html).

Roberts, S. Craig et al., *Female facial attractiveness increases during the fertile phase of the menstrual cycle*, 271 PROCEEDINGS OF THE ROYAL SOCIETY B: BIOLOGICAL SCIENCES (2004).

Roberts, Sam, *U.S. Births Hint at Bias for Boys in Some Asians*, N.Y. TIMES, Jun. 15, 2009, at A1 (www.nytimes.com/2009/06/15/nyregion/15babies.html).

Rogers, Tim, *Girl Power; Women Win Big in Costa Rica*, IN THESE TIMES, Jun. 10, 2002, at 6.

Roney, James et al., *Reading men's faces: women's mate attractiveness judgments track men's testosterone and interest in infants*, 273 PROCEEDINGS OF THE ROYAL SOCIETY B: BIOLOGICAL SCIENCES 2169-2175 (2006) (primate.uchicago.edu/2006PROC.pdf).

Rosenberg, Tina, *Talking Points: How to Fight Poverty: 8 Programs That Work*, N.Y. TIMES, Nov. 16 , 2006.

Rosin, Hanna, *The End of Men: How Women are Taking Control of Everything*, THE ATLANTIC, Jul.-Aug. 2010 (www.theatlantic.com/magazine/archive/2010/07/the-end-of-men/8135).

Ross, Brian et al., *Victim: Gang-Rape Cover-Up by U.S., Halliburton/KBR*, ABC NEWS, Dec. 10, 2007 (abcnews.go.com/Blotter/story?id=3977702).

Roter, Debra et al., *Physician Gender Effects in Medical Communication*, 288 J. AMER. MED ASS'N 756 (2002).

Rowe, David C., THE LIMITS OF FAMILY INFLUENCE: GENES, EXPERIENCE, AND BEHAVIOR (Guilford Press 1993).

Roy, Nilanjana, *The Female Factor: Fighting for Safe Passage on Indian Streets*, N.Y. TIMES, Aug. 3, 2010 (www.nytimes.com/2010/08/04/world/asia/04iht-letter.html).

Ruddick, Sara, MATERNAL THINKING: TOWARD A POLITICS OF PEACE (Beacon Press 1995 Ed.).

Ryan, Joan, Op-Ed, *Bosses not babies at issue*, S.F. CHRONICLE, Apr. 16, 2002, at A17.

—— Op-Ed, *Women, get angry*, S.F. CHRONICLE, Nov. 12, 2002, at A19.

Sadler, AG et al., *Gang and multiple rapes during military service: health consequences and health care*, 60 JOURNAL OF THE AMERICAN MEDICAL WOMEN'S ASS'N. 33 (2005).

Sands, Emily G., *Opening the Curtain on Playwright Gender: An Integrated Economic Analysis of Discrimination in American Theater*, Undergraduate Thesis submitted to Princeton Univ. Dep't of Economics, Apr. 15, 2009 (http://graphics8.nytimes.com/packages/pdf/theater/Openingthecurtain.pdf)

Sanghavi, Prachi et al., *Fire-related deaths in India in 2001: a retrospective analysis of data*, THE LANCET, Early Online Publication, 2 March 2009 doi:10.1016/S0140-6736(09)60235-X.

Sang-hun, Choe, *South Korea, Where Boys Were Kings, Revalues its Girls*, N.Y. TIMES, Dec. 23, 2007, at A1 (www.nytimes.com/2007/12/23/world/asia/23skorea.html).

Sapolsky, Robert M. & Share, Lisa J., *A Pacific Culture among Wild Baboons: Its Emergence and Transmission*, 2 PLoS BIOLOGY 534-41 (2004) (www.ncbi.nlm.nih.gov/pmc/articles/PMC387274/).

Sax, Leonard, WHY GENDER MATTERS: WHAT PARENTS AND TEACHERS NEED TO KNOW ABOUT THE EMERGING SCIENCE OF SEX DIFFERENCES (Doubleday 2005).

Schemo, Diana Jean, *4 Top Officers at Air Force Academy Are Replaced*, N.Y. TIMES, Mar. 26, 2003, at A10.

—— *Air Force Secretary Says Academy's Leaders Could Be Punished*, N.Y. TIMES, Apr. 2, 2003, at A18.

—— *Rate of Rape at Academy is Put at 12% in Survey*, N.Y. TIMES, Aug. 29, 2003, at A12.

—— *Women at West Point Face Tough Choices on Assaults*, N.Y. TIMES, May 22, 2003, at A16.

Schemo, Diana Jean, with Moss, Michael, *Criminal Charges Possible in Air Force Rape Scandal*, N.Y. TIMES, Mar. 27, 2003, at A17.

Schieman, Scott & McMullen, Taralyn, *Relational Demography in the Workplace and Health: An Analysis of Gender and the Subordinate-Superordinate Role-Set*, 49 J. HEALTH AND SOCIAL BEHAVIOR 286 (Sept. 2008).

Schmidt, Michael & Ghazi Yasir, *Iraqi Women Feel Shunted Despite Election Quota*, N.Y. TIMES, Mar. 13, 2011, at A4 (www.nytimes.com/2011/03/13/world/middleeast/13baghdad.html).

Schmitt, David et al., *Why Can't a Man Be More Like a Woman? Sex Differences in Big Five Personality Traits Across 55 Cultures*, 94 JOURNAL OF PERSONALITY AND SOCIAL PSYCHOLOGY 168 (2008) (www.bradley.edu/dotAsset/165918.pdf).

Schmitt, Eric, *Military Women Reporting Rapes by U.S. Soldiers*, N.Y. TIMES, Feb. 26, 2004, at A1.

—— *Reports of Rape in Pacific Spur Air Force Steps*, N.Y. TIMES, Mar. 9, 2004, at A1.

Schmitt, Eric with Moss, Michael, *Air Force Academy Investigated 54 Sexual Assaults in 10 Years*, N.Y. TIMES, Mar. 7, 2003, at A1.

Schroedel, Jean Reith, IS THE FETUS A PERSON?: A COMPARISON OF POLICIES ACROSS THE FIFTY STATES (Cornell Univ. Press 2000) (books.google.com/books?id=pnJzmzlOF24C).

Schumpeter: Womenomics: Feminist management theorists are flirting with some dangerous arguments, ECONOMIST, Dec. 30, 2009, at 48 (www.economist.com/businessfinance/displaystory.cfm?story_id=1517274 6).

Seelye, Katharine, *Specter Legacy Is Study of the Perils of a Switch*, N.Y. TIMES, May 23, 2010, at A14 (www.nytimes.com/2010/05/23/us/politics/23specter.html).

Seelye, Katharine Q. & Erlanger, Steven, *U.S. Suspends the Transport of Terror Suspects to Cuba*, N.Y. TIMES, Jan. 24, 2002, at A1.

Seligson, Hannah, *Preoccupations: Girl Power at School, but Not at the Office*, N.Y. TIMES, Aug. 31, 2008, at BU11 (www.nytimes.com/2008/08/31/jobs/31pre.html).

Sellers, Patricia, *Power: Do women really want it?*, FORTUNE, Oct. 13, 2003, at 80.

Sen, Amartya, *More Than 100 Million Women Are Missing*, N.Y. REV. OF BOOKS, Dec. 20, 1990 (ucatlas.ucsc.edu/gender/Sen100M.html).

Sengupta, Kim, *Disembowelled, then torn apart: The price of daring to teach girls*, THE INDEPENDENT, Nov. 29, 2006 (www.independent.co.uk/news/world/asia/disembowelled-then-torn-apart-the-price-of-daring-to-teach-girls-426241.html).

Sengupta, Somini, *For Iraqi Girls, Changing Land Narrows Lives*, N.Y. TIMES, Jun. 27, 2004, at § 1, at 1.

Shannon, Victoria, *The Female Factor: Equal Rights for Women? Survey Says: Yes, but ...*, N.Y. TIMES, Jun. 30, 2010 (www.nytimes.com/2010/07/01/world/01iht-poll.html).

Shin, Annys, *Work-life benefits fall victim to slow economy*, LA TIMES, Apr. 4, 2009 (http://articles.latimes.com/2009/apr/04/business/fi-flexible4).

Shipman, Claire & Kay, Katty, WOMENOMICS (HarperBusiness 2009).

Showlater, Elaine, THE FEMALE MALADY: WOMEN, MADNESS AND ENGLISH CULTURE, 1830-1980 (Pantheon 1985).

Siegel, Michael, *Mass Media Antismoking Campaigns*, 129 ANNALS OF INTERNAL MEDICINE 128-32 (July 15, 1998).

Simmons, Rachel, ODD GIRL OUT: THE HIDDEN CULTURE OF AGGRESSION IN GIRLS (Harcourt Brace 2002).

Sineau, Mariette, *The French Experience: Institutionalizing Parity*, in International Institute for Democracy and Electoral Assistance, WOMEN IN

PARLIAMENTS: BEYOND NUMBERS (2nd Ed. 2005)
(www.idea.int/publications/wip2).

Slackman, Michael, *A Quiet Revolution in Algeria: Gains by Women*, N.Y. TIMES, May 26, 2007, at A1.
(www.nytimes.com/2007/05/26/world/africa/26algeria.html).

Slaughter, Anne-Marie, *Why Women Still Can't Have It All*, THE ATLANTIC, Jul.-Aug. 2012
(www.theatlantic.com/magazine/archive/2012/07/why-women-still-can-t-h ave-it-all/9020/).

Slavicek, Louise, THE SALEM WITCH TRIALS: HYSTERIA IN COLONIAL AMERICA (Chelsea House Pub. 2011).

Soares, Rachel et al., *2009 Catalyst Census: Fortune 500 Women Board Directors*, Catalyst, Dec. 2009
(www.catalyst.org/file/320/2009_fortune_500_census_women_board_dire ctors.pdf).

Solimine, Michael & Wheatley, Susan, *Rethinking Feminist Judging*, 70 IND. L.J. 891 (1995).

Sommers, Christina Hoff, THE WAR AGAINST BOYS: HOW MISGUIDED FEMINISM IS HARMING OUR YOUNG MEN (Simon & Schuster 2000).

Spencer, S. et al., *Stereotype threat and women's math performance*, 35 JOURNAL OF EXPERIMENTAL SOCIAL PSYCHOLOGY, 4 (1999).

Stephan, Maria & Chenoweth, Erica, *Why Civil Resistance Works*, 33 INTERNATIONAL SECURITY 7 (2008)
(www.nonviolent-conflict.org/PDF/IS3301_pp007-044_Stephan_Chenowe th.pdf).

Stein, Rob, *Teen Birth Rate Rises in U.S., Reversing a 14-Year Decline*, WASHINGTON POST, Dec. 6, 2007, at A1
(www.washingtonpost.com/wp-dyn/content/article/2007/12/05/AR200712 0501208.html).

Stevenson, Betsey & Wolfers, Justin, *The Paradox of Declining Female Happiness*, Nat. Bur. of Economics Research Working Paper No. 14969, May 2009
(isites.harvard.edu/fs/docs/icb.topic457678.files//WomensHappiness.pdf).

Stickley, Andrew et al., *Attitudes Toward Intimate Partner Violence Against Women in Moscow, Russia*, 23 JOURNAL OF FAMILY VIOLENCE 447 (2008).

Stone, Pamela, OPTING OUT?: WHY WOMEN REALLY QUIT CAREERS AND HEAD HOME (Univ. of California Press 2007).

Strecker, Edward A, THEIR MOTHERS' SONS (Lippincott 1946).

Strier, Karen B., *Beyond the Apes: Reasons to Consider the Entire Primate Order*, *in* TREE OF ORIGIN 69-93 (Frans B. M. de Waal ed., Harvard Univ. Press 2001).

Su, Rong et al., *Men and Things, Women and People: A Meta-Analysis of Sex Differences in Interests*, 135 PSYCHOLOGICAL BULLETIN 859 (2009) (https://netfiles.uiuc.edu/jrounds/IIP/Su_Rounds_Armstrong_09.pdf).

Sullivan, Tim, *Modern India still prays for boys*, Associated Press, USA TODAY, Apr. 14, 2008 (www.usatoday.com/news/world/2008-04-13-4188616121_x.htm).

Sunstein, Cass, THE SECOND BILL OF RIGHTS: FDR'S UNFINISHED REVOLUTION AND WHY WE NEED IT MORE THAN EVER (Basic Books 2004).

Surowiecki, James, THE WISDOM OF CROWDS (Doubleday 2004).

Swers, Michele L., THE DIFFERENCE WOMEN MAKE: THE POLICY IMPACT OF WOMEN IN CONGRESS (Univ. of Chicago Press 2002).

Talbot, Margaret, *Girls Just Want to Be Mean*, N.Y. TIMES MAGAZINE, Feb. 24, 2002, at 24.

—— *A Woman's Work*, N.Y. TIMES MAGAZINE, Mar. 30, 2003, at 7.

Tanenbaum, Leora, CATFIGHT: WOMEN AND COMPETITION (Seven Stories Press 2002).

Tavris, Carol, THE MISMEASURE OF WOMAN (Simon & Schuster 1992).

Taylor, Shelley E., THE TENDING INSTINCT: HOW NURTURING IS ESSENTIAL TO WHO WE ARE AND HOW WE LIVE (Times Books 2002).

Terzieff, Juliette, *Baby Girls Fill Pakistan's Public Cradles*, WOMEN'S ENEWS, Oct. 17, 2004 (www.womensenews.org/article.cfm?aid=2031).

—— *Pakistan tries to turn tables on ignorance, extremism; Punjab revamps schools to offer high-quality, free education*, S.F. CHRONICLE, Mar. 30, 2004, at F1.

—— *'Until death do us part' is a real threat for Pakistani couple; Married pair is told to compensate family or face execution*, S.F. CHRONICLE, Jul. 25, 2004, at A3.

—— *Women's plight stirs Pakistan; High-profile cases arouse outrage against abuses of male-run society*, S.F. CHRONICLE, Aug. 4, 2002, at A15.

The smell of power: Odour and mating preferences, ECONOMIST, Jul. 7, 2005 (www.economist.com/node/4149493?story_id=4149493).

The Intelligent Investor, *For Mother's Day, Give Her Reins to the Portfolio*, WALL STREET JOURNAL, May 9, 2009, at B1 (online.wsj.com/article/SB124181915279001967.html).

Thom son, Carla, *Experts: Hottest Hip Hop Glorifies Pimping*, WOMEN'S ENEWS, Nov. 9, 2003 (www.womensenews.org/article.cfm?aid=1594).

Thurschwell, Adam, *Radical Feminist Liberalism, in* 31 IMAGINING LAW: ON DRUCILLA CORNELL (Renee Heberle & Benjamin Pryor eds., State Univ. of N.Y. Press 2008).

Tierney, John, *As Barriers Disappear, Some Gender Gaps Widen*, N.Y. TIMES, Sept. 9, 2008, at F1 (www.nytimes.com/2008/09/09/science/09tier.html).

Toobin, Jeffrey, *Women in Black; Female judges are more compassionate than men, the theory goes. Not in Texas.*, THE NEW YORKER, Oct. 30, 2000, at 48.

Torregrosa, Luisita Lopez, *The Female Factor: Evaluating Challenges Women Face*, INT'L HERALD TRIB., Mar. 7, 2012 (www.nytimes.com/2012/03/07/us/07iht-letter07.html).

—— *The Female Factor: High Hopes 2012 Will Be a Good Year for Women*, INT'L HERALD TRIB., Jan. 11, 2012 (www.nytimes.com/2012/01/11/us/11iht-letter11.html).

Trampe, Debra et al., *The Self-Activation Effect of Advertisements: Ads Can Affect Whether and How Consumers Think About the Self*, JOURNAL OF CONSUMER RESEARCH (April 2011).

Tuna, Cari & Lublin, Joann, *Welch: 'No Such Thing as Work-Life Balance'*, WALL STREET JOURNAL, Jul. 14, 2009 (http://online.wsj.com/article/SB124726415198325373.html).

Turow, Scott, ONE L (G.P. Putnam's Sons 1977).

Tyre, Peg, *The Trouble With Boys*, NEWSWEEK, Jan. 30, 2006, at 44.

UNICEF, *State of the World's Children 2004* (www.unicef.org/sowc04/files/SOWC_O4_eng.pdf).

—— *State of the World's Children 2007* (www.unicef.org/sowc07/docs/sowc07.pdf).

U.S. will undergo human rights scrutiny, WASHINGTON POST, Mar. 18, 2010 (www.washingtonpost.com/wp-dyn/content/article/2010/03/17/AR2010031704114.html).

United States Dep't of State, *The Annual Trafficking in Persons Report*, June, 2003 (www.state.gov/documents/organization/21555.pdf).

United States Gov. Accountability Office, *Gender Pay Differences: Progress Made, but Women Remain Overrepresented among Low-Wage Workers*, Oct. 2011.

Valen, Kelly, THE TWISTED SISTERHOOD: UNRAVELING THE DARK LEGACY OF FEMALE FRIENDSHIPS (Ballantine Books 2010).

Valian, Virginia, WHY SO SLOW?: THE ADVANCEMENT OF WOMEN (MIT Press 1998).

Vandermassen, Griet, WHO'S AFRAID OF CHARLES DARWIN?: DEBATING FEMINISM AND EVOLUTIONARY THEORY (Rowman & Littlefield Publishers, Inc. 2005).

Vedantam, Shankar, *Salary, Gender and the Social Cost of Haggling*, WASHINGTON POST, Jul. 30, 2007, at A7 (www.washingtonpost.com/wp-dyn/content/article/2007/07/29/AR200707 2900827.html).

Virginia: Raunchy Videos Won't Mean the End of a Captain's Navy Career, Associated Press, N.Y. TIMES, Aug. 25, 2011, at A17 (www.nytimes.com/2011/08/25/us/25brfs-Carrier.html).

Wade, Nicholas, *Darwin, Ahead of His Time, Is Still Influential*, N.Y. TIMES, Feb. 10, 2009, at D1 (www.nytimes.com/2009/02/10/science/10evolution.html).

—— *She Doesn't Trust You? Blame the Testosterone*, N.Y. TIMES, Jun. 8, 2010, at D7 (www.nytimes.com/2010/06/08/health/08hormone.html).

Wagner, Sally Roesch, MATILDA JOSLYN GAGE: SHE WHO HOLDS THE SKY (Sky Carrier Press 1998).

Warner, Judith, *Mommy Madness*, NEWSWEEK, Feb. 21, 2005, at 42.

—— PERFECT MADNESS: MOTHERHOOD IN THE AGE OF ANXIETY (Riverhead 2005).

Watson, Liz & Swanberg, Jennifer, *Flexible Workplace Solutions for Low-Wage Hourly Workers: A Framework for a National Conversation*, Workplace Flexibility 2010 at Georgetown Law, 2011 (http://workplaceflexibility2010.org/images/uploads/whatsnew/Flexible%2 0Workplace%20Solutions%20for%20Low-Wage%20Hourly%20Workers. pdf).

Webster, Murray & Driskell, James, *Beauty as Status*, 89 AMER. J. SOCIOLOGY 140 (1983).

Weisman, Steven R., *U.S. Says Evidence Confirms Reports of Mass Rapes by Burmese*, N.Y. TIMES, Dec. 27, 2002, at A7.

Weller, Robert, *Air Force kept cadet after sex charges*, Associated Press, S.F. CHRONICLE, Mar. 29, 2004, at A2.

—— *Rankling symbol comes down*, Associated Press, S.F. CHRONICLE, Mar. 31, 2003, at A19.

Wenneras, C., & Wold, A., *Nepotism and sexism in peer-review*, 387 NATURE 341 (1997).

Werdigier, Julia, *The Female Factor: Group Sets Goal to Get More Women on Boards*, N.Y. TIMES, Dec. 11, 2010 at B3 (www.nytimes.com/2010/12/11/business/global/11boards.html).

What Women Want, NEWSWEEK, Mar. 17, 2008, at 28.

White, Emily, FAST GIRLS: TEENAGE TRIBES AND THE MYTH OF THE SLUT (Scribner 2002).

Whitfield, John, *Do mammals sleep around to stick around? Hunting hits monogamous species hardest*, NAUTURE SCIENCE UPDATE, June 2, 2003.

Williams, Joan & Huang, Penelope, *Improving Work-Life Fit in Hourly Jobs: An Underutilized Cost-Cutting Strategy in a Globalized World*, The Center for WorkLife Law at Univ. Cal. Hastings College of Law, 2011 (www.worklifelaw.org/pubs/ImprovingWork-LifeFit.pdf).

Wilson, Marie C., CLOSING THE LEADERSHIP GAP: WHY WOMEN CAN AND MUST HELP RUN THE WORLD (Viking Press 2004).

Wiseman, Rosalind, QUEEN BEES AND WANNABES: HELPING YOUR DAUGHTER SURVIVE CLIQUES, GOSSIP, BOYFRIENDS AND OTHER REALITIES OF ADOLESCENCE (Crown Publishing 2002).

Wishik, Heather Ruth, *To Question Everything: The Inquiries of Feminist Jurisprudence*, 1 BERKELEY WOMEN'S LAW JOURNAL 64 (1986).

Women in Law in the U.S., Catalyst, Sept. 2009.

Women in the workforce: Female power, ECONOMIST, Dec. 30, 2009, at 49 (www.economist.com/displaystory.cfm?story_id=15174418).

Womenomics revisited, ECONOMIST, Apr. 19, 2007 (www.economist.com/node/9038760).

Women on the Front Lines of Health Care: State of the World's Mothers 2010, Save the Children (www.savethechildren.net/alliance/what_we_do/every_one/reports/SOWM 2010_Report.pdf).

Wood, Wendy & Eagly, Alice, *A Cross-Cultural Analysis of the Behavior of Women and Men: Implications for the Origins of Sex Differences*, 128 PSYCHOLOGICAL BULLETIN 699 (2002) (dornsife.usc.edu/wendywood/research/documents/Wood.Eagly.2002.pdf).

Woolls, Daniel, *Spain Lawmakers OK Women's Equality Law*, Associated Press, NEWSDAY, Mar. 15, 2007.

Wrangham, Richard W., *Out of the Pan, Into the Fire: How Our Ancestors' Evolution Depended on What They Ate*, in TREE OF ORIGIN 119-43 (Frans B. M. de Waal ed., Harvard Univ. Press 2001).

Wrangham, Richard W. & Peterson, Dale, DEMONIC MALES: APES AND THE ORIGINS OF HUMAN VIOLENCE (Houghton Mifflin Co. 1996).

Wright, Nicholas et al., *Testosterone disrupts human collaboration by increasing egocentric choices*, PROCEEDINGS OF THE ROYAL SOCIETY B (doi:10.1098/rspb.2011.2523) (http://rspb.royalsocietypublishing.org/content/early/2012/01/27/rspb.2011 .2523.full.pdf).

Yardley, Jim, *Critic Is Described as Scrupulous and Determined*, N.Y. TIMES, May 25, 2002, at A10.

Yunus, Muhammad, interview on *All Things Considered* (NPR radio broadcast, *Loan Bank Work Brings Nobel Prize to Bangladeshi*, Oct. 13, 2006).

Zernike, Kate, *Step Right Up: She Just Might Be President Someday*, N.Y. TIMES MAGAZINE, May 18, 2008. (www.nytimes.com/2008/05/18/weekinreview/18zernike.html).

Endnotes

(For access to web pages that have expired or changed, see www.archive.org)

1. Slaughter.

2. Performed by Diana Ross, ©1980 Bernard's Other Music, BMI/Sony/ATV Songs LLC.

3. Leonhardt, *Economic Scene.*

4. *10 Reasons*; Rosin.

5. Kristof, *Sentenced to Be Raped.*

6. *See* Goldstein at 252-300, 333; Braudy.

7. Jefferson (Jefferson is misquoted often about this).

8. Surowiecki,

9. Bower.

10. Brooks, David, *The Democrats Rejoice.*

11. Shipman.

12. Buckingham.

13. *E.g.*, Reich, OPPOSING THE SYSTEM.

14. *Women on the Front Lines.*

15. *Women on the Front Lines.*

16. Hausmann at 10.

17. Gentleman.

18. Gentleman.

19. Rosin.

20. *10 Reasons.*

21. *10 Reasons.*

22. Hegewisch & Williams.

23. Hegewisch et al.

24. Conlin; *see* Tyre; Sommers.

25. Rosin.

26. Miller, Claire.

27. Conlin at 82.

28. Hartmann.

29. Leonhardt, *Gender Pay Gap.*

30. Lo Sasso.

31. Carvajal.

32. Hegewisch & Williams.

33. U.S. Gov't Accountability Office.

34. *Equality in Job Loss*; Boushey.

35. Belkin, *New Gender Gap.*

36. Belkin, *New Gender Gap.*

37. Bennhold, *Recession Seen.*

38. Su (meta-analysis); Myers, D. at 162-63.

39. Hegewisch et al.

40. Hill, Catherine at 38-41.

41. Hill, Catherine at 39-40 (citing Spencer).

42. Lewin, *Bias Called Persistent* (citing Hill, Catherine).

43. Angier, *Pay Gap.*

44. Angier, *Pay Gap.*

45. Angier, *Pay Gap* (quoting Dr. Peter H. Raven) (interview).

46. Hartmann.

47. Rosin.

48. Rampell.

49. Hua.

50. Creswell.

51. Soares.

52. Chiang, *Women Still Underrepresented.*

53. Clark, Nicola.

54. Choo at 58-59.

55. *Report of the Fourth Annual National Survey.*

56. *Women in Law.*

57. Center for American Women and Politics, *Statewide Elective Executive Women.*

58. *See* Center for American Women and Politics, *Women in State Legislatures.*

59. Ryan, *Women, get Angry.*

60. Inter-Parliamentary Union.

61. Center for American Women and Politics, *Women in the U.S. Congress.*

62. Ryan, *Women, get angry.*

63. Wilson at 61-63; Moncrief at 102.

64. Lawless.

65. Eagleton Institute of Politics.

66. Corcoran.

67. Swers; Wilson at 9-11; UNICEF, *The State of the World's Children 2007, Executive Summary*, at 13.

68. Slaughter.

69. *10 Reasons.*

70. Torregrosa, *High Hopes.*

71. Wishik.

72. *E.g.*, Barnett & Rivers, SAME DIFFERENCE.

73. Brizendine at 160.

74. Dillon; Dillon & Rimer.

75. Angier & Chang (noting that high math scores are a poor predictor of choice of a scientific career); Kane & Mertz (86 nation study concluding gender differences in math performance due to cultural factors).

76. Hennessey.

77. Schumpeter.

78. Brizendine at 161.

79. Murray; Myers, D. at 60-81.

80. Brizendine at 161.

81. Cahill.

82. Schmitt, David at 169; Tierney.

83. Schmitt, David at 180.

84. Schmitt, David at 179-80.

85. Wood at 701.

86. Schmitt, David at 179-80.

87. Schmitt, David at 179.

88. Schmitt, David at 176 & 179.

89. Deaner; Schmitt, David at 179; Tierney.

90. Deaner; Schmitt, David at 179; Tierney.

91. Guinier at 99-100 & n.272 (citing Littleton at 1280). Guinier was President Clinton's first appointee to head the Civil Rights Division of the Justice Department, but her nomination was withdrawn in the face of conservative opposition – in part due to her support for using proportional representation in the election of public officials.

92. Landesman, *A Woman's Work.*

93. McKinley, James.

94. *E.g.*, Barnett & Rivers, SAME DIFFERENCE at 134-42.

95. Butterfield.

96. Conlin at 79; Baron-Cohen at 35-41.

97. Fisher, THE FIRST SEX at 158 (citing a nine-to-one ratio in the incidence of violence by males versus females).

98. Butterfield (noting women surpassed men at embezzlement starting in the mid-1990s).

99. Baron-Cohen at 36 (citing Daly & Wilson).

100. Baron-Cohen at 36.

101. Myers, D. at 109.

102. National Center for Women & Policing.

103. *2001 Report of the Independent Auditor*.

104. Bonner.

105. Dawkins.

106. Wade, *Darwin*.

107. Wade, *Darwin*.

108. Wade, *Darwin*.

109. Wade, *Darwin*.

110. Vandermassen.

111. Hrdy, MOTHER NATURE 36

112. Archibold.

113. Hrdy, MOTHER NATURE at 194-96, 104-05.

114. *Id.* at 361-62.

115. *See* Hrdy, MOTHER NATURE at 80-83.

116. Vandermassen; Buss & Schmitt..

117. Hrdy, MOTHER NATURE at 329-35 (citing Trivers-Willard hypothesis).

118. Mathews.

119. *E.g.*, Arnqvist & Rowe; Angier, *Men, Women, Sex And Darwin*.

120. Baron-Cohen at 125; Wrangham & Peterson at 233-34.

121. Angier, *Is War Our Biological Destiny?*

122. Wrangham & Peterson at 232-36.

123. Haughney.

124. Pinker at 345; *see* Darwinawards.com.

125. Wrangham & Peterson at 239.

126. *See* Wrangham & Peterson at 239 & n.8; Fisher, THE FIRST SEX at 41-42 (linking testosterone with the urge to fight for rank).

127. Kolata.

128. Brizendine at 14.

129. Gettler.

130. Brizendine at 25.

131. Wade, *She Doesn't Trust You?*

132. Wright.

133. Wrangham & Peterson at 184 n.

134. Wrangham & Peterson at 183-85.

135. Wrangham & Peterson at 156, 160 (noting that outside males lions often murder when they take over a pride).

136. Komisaruk at 17.

137. (citing research by Behavioral Health Professor Laura Cousino Klein).

138. Fagan.

139. Taylor.

140. Hall, *Study finds genetic link to violence* (citing twenty-five-year study of 442 New Zealand boys).

141. *Id.*

142. Hrdy, MOTHER NATURE at 564 n.39 (citing both Ember and Murdock).

143. Hrdy, MOTHER NATURE at 238; Pinker at 319.

144. Wrangham & Peterson at 67, 78 (describing the South American Yanomamö, Waorani and Quichua).

145. Stephan at 8-9.

146. Tavris at 70-71.

147. Talbot, *A Woman's Work.*

148. Talbot, *A Woman's Work.*

149. Barnett & Rivers, SAME DIFFERENCE at 135-37 (citing Lightdale).

150. Barnett & Rivers, *Abu Ghraib Pulls 'Better Angels' Down to Earth.*

151. Roter at 761-63.

152. Stevenson.

153. *Id.* at 1.

154. *Id.* at 4, 17.

155. *Id.* at 5, 19-20. West Germany was the only exception.

156. Buckingham.

157. Stevenson at 2.

158. *Id.* at 3.

159. *Id.* at 22-23.

160. Schmitt, David at 172.

161. Schmitt, David at 176 & 179.

162. Slavicek.

163. Freud & Breuer.

164. Maines.

165. Showlater.

166. *See* Flanagan.

167. Slaughter.

168. Nance-Nash, *Fewer Employers.*

169. Shin.

170. May, Elaine.

171. Stone.

172. Shipman.

173. Tuna.

174. Gootman.

175. *Women in the workforce* at 50; Bertrand at 8.

176. Bertrand at 25.

177. Horton-Flaherty at 20.

178. Horton-Flaherty at 20.

179. Anderson, J. (quoting sixth-year associate in Los Angeles office of Philadelphia-based law firm).

180. *E.g.*, Brooks, Arthur at 62-75.

181. *E.g.*, Stevenson at 17-18.

182. Ryan, *Bosses not babies* (citing Hewlett, CREATING A LIFE).

183. Ryan, *Bosses not babies* (citing study by Mary Ann Mason, UC Berkeley Dean of the Graduate Division).

184. Noer.

185. Hewlett, OFF RAMPS; Belkin, *New Gender Gap*.

186. McGinn at 64.

187. McGinn at 64.

188. Belkin, *Motherlode*.

189. McGinn at 66.

190. McGinn at 64.

191. Belkin, *New Gender Gap*.

192. *Equality in Job Loss*; Boushey.

193. Miller, Kevin (using U.S. Dep't of Ed. data).

194. *Womenomics revisited*.

195. *See* Bernard.

196. *Womenomics revisited*.

197. Stevenson at 5, 19-20. West Germany was the only exception.

198. Seligson.

199. Sellers at 88.

200. Babcock.

201. Vedantam.

202. Clark, Heather.

203. Valian.

204. Desvaux.

205. Clark, Nicola (quoting Benja Stig-Fagerland).

206. Valen at 122-23.

207. *A guide to womenomics.*

208. Ferrary.

209. *See* Evans, G., SHE WINS at ix-x.

210. *See* Fisher, THE FIRST SEX at 43-44; Chesler; Tanenbaum; Seligson; Klaus; Valen; Batlan.

211. Schieman.

212. Baer at 17 (citing MacKinnon at 47-48).

213. Evans, G., SHE WINS at 15.

214. *See* Evans, G., SHE WINS at 7, 158-62.

215. Klaus.

216. Myers, D. at 158.

217. Costello-Dougherty.

218. Creswell.

219. Littleton at 1302 (emphasis in original), *quoted in* Tavris at 108.

220. Guinier at 4.

221. Guinier at 5.

222. Guinier at 49 n.122, 71.

223. Guinier at 4 (emphasis and alteration in original).

224. Guinier at 46 n.116.

225. Turow at 220, *quoted in* Baer at 75.

226. Kristof, *Turning Oppression*.

227. Talbot, *Girls Just Want to Be Mean* (quoting Elizabeth Fox-Genovese) (interview).

228. Chesler; Simmons (describing "the facade of female intimacy" covering "the hidden culture of aggression"); White, E.; Wiseman (refering to "Alpha Girls" and "Really Mean Girls").

229. Paul.

230. Talbot, *Girls Just Want to Be Mean* (quoting Kaj Bjorkqvist) (emphasis added) (interview).

231. Talbot, *Girls Just Want to Be Mean* (quoting Kaj Bjorkqvist) (interview).

232. Talbot, *Girls Just Want to Be Mean* (quoting Marion Underwood of the University of Texas at Dallas).

233. Cohen, Patricia.

234. Sands at 55.

235. Sands at 65-66.

236. Sands at 77.

237. Sands at 64.

238. Sands at 87-102.

239. Hill, Catherine at 24-25 (citing Wenneras).

240. Sands at 80-83.

241. Braw.

242. James.

243. Valen at 142-58.

244. Angier, *No Time for Bullies*; Sapolsky.

245. Angier, *No Time for Bullies*; Sapolsky.

246. Bennhold, *20 Years After Fall*.

247. Bennhold, *20 Years After Fall*.

248. Bennhold, *20 Years After Fall*.

249. Bennhold, *20 Years After Fall*.

250. Angier, *Is War Our Biological Destiny?*

251. Gettleman, *Rwanda*; Polgreen.

252. Clark, Nicola.

253. Clark, Nicola.

254. Werdigier.

255. Buzek.

256. Kramer, Vicki; Creswell; *see 2005 Catalyst Census*.

257. Soares.

258. Clark, Nicola, (citing Desvaux).

259. *Beauty and success*; Hamermesh; Etcoff et al.

260. Miller-Medzon (citing Etcoff); Fisher, The First Sex at 234. *But see* Barnett & Rivers, Same Difference at 71-74 (criticizing 1989 global study).

261. Etcoff et al.

262. McKinley, Jesse.

263. Webster.

264. Kuchment.

265. Kristof, *Turning Oppression*.

266. Levy.

267. Deveny, *Girls Gone Bad?*

268. Levy.

269. *Quoted in* Bergner, *What Do Women Want?*.

270. Strier at 92.

271. Wrangham, *Out of the Pan* at 135.

272. Brizendine at 88.

273. Parker-Pope.

274. Cultures of Multiple Fathers, *cited in* Lehrman.

275. *E.g.*, Angier, *Men, Women, Sex And Darwin*.

276. Fisher, THE FIRST SEX at 266 (citing Morell).

277. Gangestad (finding more than a 65% increase in extra-partner fantasies during ovulation among students at the Univ. of New Mexico).

278. Roberts, S. Craig.

279. *Playing Away* (reporting on research by Gangestad).

280. Gangestad.

281. Strier at 88.

282. Miller & Maner.

283. Penton-Voak.

284. Little (noting that high masculinity correlates with decreased paternal care of offspring); *see* Duenwald, *For a Good Time* (comparing the appeal of cads vs. dads); *Oochy woochy* (citing Roney).

285. *The smell of power* (citing Havlicek).

286. Myers, Steven L., *Another Peril*.

287. Goldstein at 332-79.

288. Moss (discussing controversy over Defense Department Advisory Committee on Women in the Services).

289. Moffeit.

290. Sadler.

291. www.mentalhealth.va.gov/msthome.asp

292. Moffeit.

293. Schmitt, *Reports of Rape in Pacific*.

294. Moffeit.

295. Schmitt, *Military Women Reporting Rapes*.

296. Gibbs.

297. *Defense Task Force*.

298. *Military Personnel*.

299. Myers, Steven L., *Another Peril*.

300. Gibbs.

301. Myers, Steven L., *Another Peril*.

302. *Military Personnel*.

303. *Defense Task Force*.

304. Ross.

305. Janofsky, *General Asks Air Force*.

306. Janofsky with Schemo.

307. Janofsky with Schemo.

308. Janofsky, *Air Force Begins an Inquiry*.

309. Janofsky with Schemo.

310. Weller, *Air Force*.

311. Schemo, *Air Force Secretary Says*.

312. Janofsky, *Air Force Begins an Inquiry*.

313. *See* Reid; Jargon (Denver weekly newspaper broke the story and followed it throughout 2003).

314. *See* Reid.

315. Schemo, *Women at West Point*.

316. Koopman.

317. Moss; Weller, *Rankling symbol* (describing removal of the sign after a rape scandal embarrassed the Academy).

318. Schemo, *4 Top Officers* (quoting Andrea Prasse, who accused another cadet of sexual harassment).

319. Bumiller.

320. *Virginia: Raunchy Videos.*

321. Ruddick at 143-45.

322. Parker, Ashley.

323. Kraft.

324. *See* Brown (interview with feminist Gloria Steinem).

325. Seelye & Erlanger.

326. Roper v. Simmons, 543 U.S. 551 (2005).

327. Greenhouse.

328. Seelye & Erlanger.

329. Kristof, *Women's Rights.*

330. www.un.org/womenwatch/daw/cedaw.

331. Kristof, *Bush vs. Women.*

332. Omang; Editorial, *How Bush Treats Women.*

333. Omang.

334. Marquis.

335. Lederer.

336. www.unicef.org/crc/.

337. *U.S. will undergo.*

338. Torregrosa, *Evaluating Challenges.*

339. Badkhen & Haas.

340. Constable, P.

341. Fathi; Badkhen & Haas; Constable, P.; Sengupta, S.

342. Schmidt.

343. Fang.

344. Amnesty International, *Afghanistan*; Badkhen.

345. Gall (noting that only Sierra Leone, Angola and Niger have higher infant mortality rates).

346. Lamb.

347. Sengupta, Kim.

348. Boone.

349. Editorial, *Window of Opportunity.*

350. Dowden.

351. Sanghavi.

352. *See* Patten at 210-20 (describing African women's lack of basic rights, especially within marriage).

353. Hrdy, MOTHER NATURE at 325.

354. Hrdy, MOTHER NATURE at 321.

355. Hrdy, MOTHER NATURE at 322-27.

356. Prasad.

357. Jha.

358. Jones, M.

359. *See* Terzieff, *Baby Girls.*

360. Prasad.

361. Sullivan.

362. Hrdy, MOTHER NATURE at 319.

363. Prasad.

364. LaFraniere.

365. Hrdy, MOTHER NATURE at 319.

366. LaFraniere.

367. Roberts, Sam.

368. Sen.

369. Croll.

370. Oster.

371. Oster at 1164-65.

372. Prasad (quoting Andrea den Boer).

373. Hudson.

374. Sang-Hun.

375. Terzieff, *Women's plight* (noting one daughter was 5, and another, age 14, was wedded to a 55 year old).

376. Terzieff, *'Until death do us part.'*

377. Bennet.

378. Hockstader (noting that the only death other than hers was an eighty-one year old man, but over a hundred were injured).

379. Myers, Steven, *From Dismal Chechnya.*

380. Kramer, Andrew.

381. Haugen; U.S. Dep't of State; *see* Landesman, *The Girls Next Door.*

382. Kristof, *Girls for Sale.*

383. Kristof, *Modern Slavery.*

384. Koppel (citing UNICEF, *The State of the World's Children 2004*).

385. Debbie Stoller, Editor in Chief of *Bust* magazine, *quoted in* Kuczynski.

386. Stein, *Teen Birth Rate.*

387. Hegewisch & Williams.

388. www.MentorHer.com.

389. Jacoby.

390. Brooks, David, *The Tea Party Teens.*

391. Kornbluh at 111.

392. Nance-Nash, *Fewer Employers.*

393. *See* Nusbaum (describing stigma of part time work at law firms).

394. Choo at 60.

395. Hegewisch & Gornick.

396. Kulish.

397. Ryan, *Bosses not babies.*

398. Ryan, *Bosses not babies.*

399. Bennhold, *Working (Part-Time).*

400. Resnik at 661.

401. www.dti.gov.uk/employment/empl oyment-legislation/employment-gu idance/page35662.html.

402. Grainger & Holt, at 301.

403. Clark, Nicola.

404. Hegewisch & Gornick at 9; http://eur-lex.europa.eu/LexUriSer v/LexUriServ.do?uri=CELEX:319 97L0081:EN:HTML.

405. Hegewisch & Gornick at 9.

406. Ceci.

407. Cal. Gov't Code §§ 19996.19-26.

408. Hegewisch & Gornick at 18-19.

409. *See* Bennhold, *Feminism of the Future*.

410. Bennhold, *In Sweden*.

411. Bennhold, *In Sweden*.

412. Slaughter.

413. Giridharadas.

414. Williams, Joan at 3.

415. Williams, Joan at 16.

416. Williams, Joan at 10-23.

417. Williams, Joan at 25.

418. Williams, Joan at 26.

419. *Id.* at 27-49; *see* Watson.

420. Hegewisch & Gornick at 14.

421. Kornbluh at 111.

422. Hrdy, MOTHER NATURE at 508; *see* Warner, *Mommy Madness*; Warner, PERFECT MADNESS.

423. Bennhold, *In Germany*.

424. Kirp. *But see* Kristof, *How to Raise* (describing even better childhood intervention programs).

425. *See* Nance-Nash, *Fewer Employers*.

426. Fisher, THE FIRST SEX at 148-49 (discussing women's micro banks).

427. Fisher, THE FIRST SEX at 54 (citing Ho); Growthink Research (discussing need for more venture capital for women).

428. Duff-Brown.

429. Editorial, *The Hypocrisy of Farm Subsidies*.

430. Rosenberg.

431. Dugger, *In Africa, Free Schools*.

432. Terzieff, *Pakistan tries to turn tables*.

433. Koppel (citing remarks by UNICEF Executive Director Carol Bellamy).

434. Dugger, *African Studies*.

435. Editorial, *A Promising Preventive*.

436. Kristof & Wudunn.

437. Oster & Thornton.

438. Slackman.

439. Kristof, *Sentenced to Be Raped*.

440. Revkin, Andrew, *Gore Group*.

441. Wilson at 120-23.

442. Bennett.

443. Wilson at 129.

444. Wilson at 124-26 (partly blaming the foreign markets' film genre preferences).

445. Machacek.

446. Zernike.

447. Wilson at 127.

448. McNeil.

449. Hoffman, Saul.

450. *See* Laurence at 2 (1% of 67 billion).

451. Polansky at 5 (lists all films, analyzed by studio); *see* Heredia (reporting on Polansky and Dalton).

452. Dalton.

453. Polansky at 13 (recommending an R rating for any films depicting smoking).

454. Polansky at 3.

455. www.ftc.gov/opa/2003/06/2001cig rpt.htm (2001 figure reported by the Federal Trade Commission).

456. www.tobaccofreeca.com.

457. Siegel.

458. California Department of Health Services, 2006, at 2.

459. Gladwell at 216-43; Siegel.

460. Pechmann at 6.

461. See Harris; Rowe; Pinker at 372-99.

462. Pechmann.

463. Schmitt, David at 179-80.

464. See Baer at 176.

465. Faludi at 349, *quoted in* Baer at 64.

466. Faludi at 349, *quoted in* Baer at 64.

467. Michel.

468. Wilson at 103-04 (citing Kimmel); email reply to author from Dr. Kimmel, Department of Sociology, S.U.N.Y at Stony Brook (Jun. 29, 2004).

469. Ford (citing the National Crime Prevention Council).

470. National Crime Prevention Council (web.archive.org/web/2003020710 4917/http://www.ncpc.org/ncpc/nc pc/?pg=5878-5886-6652).

471. Hu.

472. www.futureswithoutviolence.org/s ection/our_work/men_and_boys.

473. Engel.

474. *See* Ruddick at 32 (citing Strecker).

475. Valen at 142-58.

476. Paul.

477. *See* Bennhold, *Feminism of the Future.*

478. Bennhold, *Working (Part-Time).*

479. Bradd Shore, Professor of Anthropology at Emery University, in panel discussion at American Anthropological Ass'n annual conference, Wash., D.C., Nov. 28, 2001.

480. Kristof, *Bush vs. Women.*

481. Terzieff, *Women's plight; see* Polk at 379-85 (describing *hudood* laws and noting that half the women in Pakistani prisons are accused of having had extramarital sex).

482. Black at 1.

483. Nebesar.

484. Hendricks.

485. Boustany.

486. Weisman.

487. Landesman, *A Woman's Work.*

488. *Ban leads call.*

489. Gettleman, *Rapes Total.*

490. Curphey; *see* Amnesty International, *Broken bodies.*

491. Roy, *Fighting for Safe Passage.*

492. Gettleman, *Fighting Congo's Ills.*

493. *See, e.g.,* Brown v. Plata, 131 S. Ct. 1910 (2011); Lewin, *Little Sympathy*; *Anomaly or Epidemic.*

494. Ruddick at 235.

495. Haidt.

496. Swers (policy priorities of women in Congress).

497. Yunus.

498. The Intelligent Investor.

499. Sunstein; *see also* Denvir.

500. Hausmann at 10.

501. *See* Duflo.

502. Fukuyama.

503. Belkin, *What's Good.*

504. Myers, D. at 240.

505. Farah.

506. Swers; Wilson at 9-11; UNICEF, *The State of the World's Children 2007, Executive Summary*, at 13.

507. Dagher.

508. Myers, D. at 234-35.

509. Gettleman, *Rwanda*; Polgreen.

510. International Institute for Democracy; *see* www.quotaproject.org.

511. UNICEF, *The State of the World's Children 2007,* at 80.

512. Donnelly (noting that Agacinski is often compared to Hillary Rodham Clinton); *see* Agacinski.

513. Sineau.

514. Woolls.

515. Rogers; www.quotaproject.org (Int'l IDEA)..

516. *See* Inter-Parliamentary Union.

517. Kristof, *The Happiest People.*

518. Ridge.

519. www.onlinewomeninpolitics.org/nz/nzmain.htm.

520. Clark, Nicola.

521. Center for American Women and Politics, *Women in State Legislatures.*

522. UNICEF, *The State of the World's Children 2007, Executive Summary*, at 12.

523. Michaels.

524. Center for American Women and Politics, *Women State Legislators: Leadership Positions and Committee Chairs.*

525. United States v. Virginia, 518 U.S. 515, 532-33 & n.6 (1996) (using intermediate rather than strict scrutiny to find unconstitutional gender discrimination at Virginia Military Institute); Adarand Constructors v. Pena, 515 U.S. 200, 247 (1995) (Stevens, J., dissenting) (noting courts evaluate gender discrimination using intermediate scrutiny and race discrimination using strict scrutiny) (citing Associated General Contractors of

Cal., Inc. v. San Francisco, 813 F.2d 922 (9th Cir. 1987) (striking down racial preference under strict scrutiny while upholding gender preference under intermediate scrutiny)). Reed v. Reed, 404 U.S. 71, 73 (1971), was the first case in which a woman alleging gender-based denial of equal protection was able to prevail in the Supreme Court. Virginia, 518 U.S. at 532.

526. Seelye.

527. Collins, *McCain's Baked Alaska*.

528. Hass at 56.

529. Collins, *My Favorite August*.

530. Gage's final editorial in the *National Citizen and Ballot Box*, *quoted in* Wagner at 67.

531. Barnett & Rivers, Same Difference at 27-28.

532. Barnett & Rivers, Same Difference at 28.

533. Toobin (citing Solimine & Wheatley).

534. Toobin.

535. Solimine & Wheatley at 897-906.

536. Toobin.

537. Toobin (quoting Solimine) (interview).

538. Solimine & Wheatley at 919.

539. Solimine & Wheatley at 918 (citing O'Connor, S. at 1549).

540. Toobin.

541. Peresie at 1767-68.

542. Peresie at 1771-76.

543. Peresie at 1776-77.

544. Peresie at 1769.

545. Peresie at 1768.

546. Peresie at 1768, 1782.

547. Peresie at 1768.

548. Peresie at 1778-79.

549. Peresie at 1781-86.

550. Dowd.

551. Yardley (noting her position as General Counsel of the Minneapolis FBI office).

552. Lacayo.

553. Sherron Watkins, *quoted in* Lacayo (alteration in original) (interview).

554. Ruddick at 225 (quoting Rich).

555. Sociology Professor Barbara Reskin, *quoted in* Chiang, *Women speak up*.

556. Watkins, *quoted in* Lacayo (interview).

557. Hill, Anita (woman who during his Supreme Court confirmation hearing accused nominee Clarence Thomas of sexual harassment).

List of Text Boxes

Acknowledgments

Sheila Jones was the girl next door in high school. She was the first feminist I knew and my gateway to progressive thinking. A free and creative spirit, she lived her beliefs without compromise. Tragically, her life was cut short by intimate partner violence. I hope the world imagined in this book is one she would have chosen, inspired in part by my conversations with Charles Reich, author of *The Greening of America*, a book Sheila adored.

As an eleven year project, this book took several forms along the way. I want to acknowledge the professors whose guidance was invaluable: John Denvir, Peter Jan Honigsberg, Shauna Marshall, Francis Neely and Charles Reich. Detailed editing and encouragement from Beth Rogozinski and Elizabeth Miles Waring helped me create a readable manuscript. An earlier version evolved only because of the helpful comments from Mike Barton, Jeff Burns, April Dembosky, Dr. Alicia Dustira, Bettina Duval, Anne Erwin, Dr. Dave Erwin, Linda Levenson, David Long, Armistead Maupin, Art Murphy, Jill Okimoto, Rachel Pusey, Dr. Sarah Stanley, Sari Steel, Louise Vance, Dr. Jarrett Walker, Dabney Waring, and especially from Deirdre Bourdet and Pamela Ostroff. Lastly, Katy Duren, Phil Ladew, Angie Miles, Dr. Charles Miles, Dr. Phil Miles, Meg Schiller, Sarah Schiller and Dabney Waring helped fine tune the final draft, and Laurie Moyal pushed me to get it out the door.

The cartoons appear through the generous permission of Women's eNews.

Index

You also can "search inside this book" at
http://amzn.com/1475292945